# VIETNAM IN THE MUD

# VIETNAM

# IN THE MUD

BY JAMES H. PICKERELL
WITH AN INTRODUCTION BY
MALCOLM W. BROWNE

THE BOBBS-MERRILL COMPANY, INC.
*A Subsidiary of Howard W. Sams & Co., Inc.*
Publishers · Indianapolis · New York · Kansas City

# CONTENTS

The photographs of the air strike in Vietnam are reprinted by courtesy of *Aviation Week & Space Technology*.

*Designed by Harsh–Finegold*
*Printed in the United States of America*

# ILLUSTRATIONS

Photographs by the author
illustrating the text will be
found following pages 12 and 76.

*. . . that from these honored dead*

*we take increased devotion to that*

*cause for which they here gave the*

*last full measure of devotion; that*

*we here highly resolve that these*

*dead shall not have died in vain; . . .*

Abraham Lincoln
Gettysburg
19 November 1863

# INTRODUCTION

It is conceivable that the United States will win its war in Vietnam by overlaying this unhappy little country with radioactive debris and killing its 30-million-odd inhabitants. It is even possible that the United States will one day elect to deal with the greater threat of China by means of nuclear holocaust, wiping out somewhere near one-quarter of the human race.

Carried to their logical conclusions, these are the directions of current American policy in Asia, notably in Vietnam.

Tragically few of our American leaders have informed themselves at first hand of the state of affairs in Asia. There are many congressional junkets, of course, but these seldom shed any light. The congressional visitor to Asia will be thoroughly briefed by his embassy, his nation's top local military officials and the host nation's top politicians. He will come back to Washington having had no more first-hand contact with the nation under study than if he had never left the United States. Senator Mike Mansfield of Montana is one of the notable exceptions to this pattern, and one of the few scholars on Asia to hold high positions in government.

Apart from this tiny minority of statesmen who are genuinely informed about things like Vietnam, there remain only some local observers here in Vietnam who have dug for the facts by themselves.

Of these, I rank the news correspondents by far the best informed and most potent. In recent years the free American press has emerged as a kind of third force in international affairs. The ability to wield a spotlight is power in itself, and I for one feel this power is a proper function of the free press.

An outstanding example of this force at its best is Jim Pickerell, who has here given us a book certain to raise hackles in official quarters. Jim tells us in effect that the Viet Cong has outsmarted the greatest industrial power on earth, which, having been bested by brains, must resort to brawn. It is an ugly picture. No American likes to imagine himself as the ugly Goliath being slain by a sickly, undernourished, Asian David. Americans, whose sense of fair play is second to none, dislike even more the image of their bad-guy Goliath finally winning, but doing so through the use of the ultimate in dirty pool—"nukes."

Sadly, there are those in our profession of journalism who extract the bulk of their news from the briefing rooms of officials in Washington and Saigon. These are the tame newsmen who deserve to be spat on by the likes of Jim Pickerell.

No man who has not seen and suffered and felt a war deserves to write about it. Jim has richly seen and suffered and felt. He came here to Vietnam with no preconceived notions, but rather with a sense of humility that distinguishes the really worthy newsman or scientist from the rest of the pack.

He has been tempered in the fires of one of the ugliest wars the United States has ever fought, and his views deserve to be heard, despite the unpleasantness of their tone. You, American reader, you have been warned.

I have worked repeatedly in the field with Jim and can vouch for his complete honesty, his great technical and artistic skill and his courage in the face of death. In the main, I entirely support his conclusions about the war.

I hope only that contributions of this kind are not too late. I hope that the work of Jim and the others here who have sought to sound the alarm will not in the end have been in vain.

*Malcolm W. Browne*
*February 1966*
*Saigon*

# FOREWORD

This book is my opinion of what is happening in Vietnam; what mistakes are being made; and what results can be expected if we continue to maintain our present Vietnam policies. I have tried to support this opinion with statistics and facts wherever possible, but in almost no instance do I consider the arguments presented to be indisputable. I have not, for the most part, tried to disprove possible counter-arguments, because in most cases there are not enough facts available on either side of the argument to come to any indisputable conclusions. Thus, I have considered the intellectual exercise of trying to disprove counter-arguments on the subject to be useless and confusing.

While there are volumes of statistical information collected in Vietnam every day, there are few unquestionable facts because there is an equal amount of pertinent information that is impossible to collect because of the nature of the war. For example, it is virtually impossible to produce an accurate sample of peasant attitudes in Viet Cong controlled areas, and yet the attitude changes of the peasants are the most important measure of our success or failure in Vietnam.

Also, the validity of certain basic statistics that are collected is often questionable. When a district chief gives a figure for refugees in his district it is often not the result of an actual count by him or a member of his staff. Rather, he simply goes to the local market place, glances around and says, "Hmm, it looks like there are about 2,000 more people here today than usual.

Must be refugees." Another example of inaccurate statistics is the now infamous "body count" that is supposed to list, by an actual count of bodies, the number of confirmed enemy killed. In actual fact, it has come to be something quite different. The Viet Cong often pull their dead off the battlefield while the battle is going on or before Americans can get sufficient control of the battlefield to be bothered with counting bodies. Nevertheless, the commanders in headquarters need a body count, and refuse to accept the fact that there may be only one or two bodies left after a heavy engagement in which obviously many were killed. These armchair commanders demand a figure that is more in line with what they think happened in the battlefield. Consequently, troops in the field have started turning in what they refer to as a SWAG count, but what their superiors still call a body count. (SWAG stands for "Stupid Wild-Ass Guess.")

All journalists realize that they cannot just report facts in such a situation, and yet most feel that there are strong ethical restrictions on their right to judge and interpret these facts. Consequently, things like body counts are still reported. Many feel that they must report everything that is presented as fact by an "official spokesman" unless they have proof that the statement is incorrect. Failure to do this, they feel, destroys their credibility as an impartial reporter. Competition, deadlines and difficulty in checking statistics given by "official spokesmen" often lead to reports that are proved incorrect within a few days.

This often makes members of the press or various publications appear irresponsible, but it seems to be a necessary and unavoidable hazard if there is to be any spot news coming out of Vietnam, or for that matter, if there is to be any coverage that is not complete, individual interpretation. I have avoided this confusion by accepting only those facts that I believe to be true and by interpreting them in a way that seems to make sense to me. This, of course, has the defect of being solely my opinion and being unprovable.

The ideas presented here have been developed as a result of widely scattered interviews, personal experiences, and impressions derived from these experiences. Many are of the type that would never be used by a good reporter because they cannot be proved and high officials are willing to make public statements claiming that there is evidence to disprove them.

I feel that contemporary reporting often fails to give a complete picture of how the various aspects of the Vietnam situation relate to one another, and this is one thing I have tried to do in this book. All of my chapter subjects have been reported on in much more depth in other media in the United States, but I think it is often difficult for the reader who finds these reports in different places, on different days, by different people, to place them in the proper perspective. While my perspective may not be the proper or only one, at least it may give the reader a better basis on which to judge the daily newspaper and magazine reports on specific aspects of the war.

Some readers may immediately wonder how I can present a complete picture of the Vietnam situation without discussing the activities in North Vietnam and their relation to the war. I leave this out because I feel it is not pertinent, nor ever has been, to solving the problems in South Vietnam. I think it would be possible to completely destroy North Vietnam, and still do very little toward solving the problems in the South or ending the war here. In fact, this may be exactly the direction in which we are heading, but I, personally, am more interested in trying to find a solution to South Vietnam's problems than in trying to guess how far we can extend the war. Our activities in North Vietnam are pertinent to the discussion only to the degree that they distract our interest from the major problem—South Vietnam. There may be other aspects of the war that I have left undiscussed, but this is because I have felt that they are minor or not pertinent at this time to the question of U.S. victory or defeat in South Vietnam.

In covering the war as a free-lance magazine photographer, I have had certain advantages over many of my colleagues. My assignments have kept me constantly on the move up and down the country, and not tied to any one particular base for a long period of time. As a result, I have probably done more traveling in Vietnam than all but a handful of reporters. The stories I cover are mostly features, rather than "spot news," and thus, I have been able to devote my time to looking at details of the overall situation while others worry about reporting the most important day-to-day happenings.

I cover the war from the level of the foot soldier, as all photographers must, because this is where the pictures are. My sources are almost exclusively men at the lowest level—captains, lieutenants, sergeants. Thus, while I may not have clearly understood the high-level plans, I have been closely associated with the men who have tried to make these plans work. Through this close association, I think I have come to understand why certain plans have succeeded and others failed. I may have had the misfortune to witness all the failures, and few successes, and therefore, the reason for my pessimistic outlook. My only argument for thinking this is not the case is that my research has been spread over a period of more than two years, and my conclusions do not seem too far out of line with some of those voiced by other correspondents who have spent many months or years in Vietnam.

The pictures in this book are those of a journalist. I feel there is seldom a story that can be completely told in pictures, and that pictures should be selected first for their story-telling qualities and secondly for their artistic value. Pictures should be used to illustrate or reinforce an idea in the text, and this often requires using a photograph that is weak in artistic qualities, but pertinent to information given in the text. I have tried to keep this in mind while selecting pictures for this book. It is not designed to be a collection of my best photographs, although many of my best are among those produced here.

Lest the reader have doubt, I would like to make it perfectly clear that I am firmly in favor of continuing the war in Vietnam. I think that there is a need for new tactics, and that present tactics will only lead to failure, but I am not advocating, in any way, that we should get out of Vietnam. I think it is still possible to win in South Vietnam if we begin to direct our actions (rather than just high-level Washington talk) toward more economic and social development for the peasants and less military hardware. I also believe that anything short of total victory will eventually be viewed in the eyes of the world as total defeat. In ten or twenty years, such a defeat may prove to have been the beginning of disaster for the American people. If we lose in Vietnam we will soon be fighting somewhere else and we will continue this fight until either we learn how to defeat the guerrillas, or there is nothing in the world left for them to win. I prefer to learn now.

In writing this book I have not tried to remain objective or hide my prejudices concerning the war. I have tried to state my beliefs as clearly as possible and to do as Leo Tolstoy recommended in his essay "The Power of Truth." He said, "It is only needful that each individual should say what he really feels or thinks, or at least that he should not say what he does not think."

This book would not have been possible without the thousands of Vietnamese and American soldiers, sailors, and airmen who helped me to move around Vietnam, to get out on special operations, and to get a first-hand impression of how the war is being fought. No words can show my appreciation for this assistance, and I only hope I have treated these men justly in this book.

I am grateful to my agent, Black Star Publishing Company, whose picture assignments have made it possible for me to stay in Vietnam.

My gratitude also goes to the many members of the Saigon foreign press corps who have so often assisted me in getting my stories. Their tips, background briefings, and the sharing of their own personal experiences have been invaluable to me as a free-lance photographer who must operate without the backing and logistical support of a large wire service, newspaper or magazine. In this sense, I must especially thank all the members of the Saigon bureau of The Associated Press and particularly Peter Arnett, Horst Faas, John Wheeler and Edwin

White, whose constant guidance and support, from the time I first arrived in Vietnam, have been so generous and so important.

A special thanks goes to Malcolm Browne for his introduction and for his aid and encouragement throughout my stay here.

I would also like to thank my mother, Mrs. Frances Pickerell, who typed the manuscript, and Henry Steiner, who selected the pictures and helped with the layout.

Finally, I would like to acknowledge the contribution of my wife, Dolly. Her endless encouragement and untiring assistance made this book possible. Without her many sacrifices it would have never been completed.

*James H. Pickerell*
*June 1966*
*Saigon*

# 1: THE AMERICAN SOLDIER

During their first nine months in Vietnam United States combat units have probably done just as much to increase the number of Communist sympathizers in South Vietnam as they have done to decrease them. As a military force, the U.S. troops are effective with their weapons, have a great deal of firepower at their disposal, and are highly trained in the use of conventional tactics in warfare. And though they usually arrive in Vietnam, after gruelling months in United States and Okinawan training camps, convinced that they are more than a match for any guerrillas, it takes only one battle like those at Plei Me, the Ira Drang Valley, or the Michelin Rubber Plantation to prove to them that the Viet Cong's fighting abilities are at least worthy of respect. In the field, the average American soldier seems to lack the endurance under hardship that is characteristic of the Viet Cong, though this is primarily because he has never experienced any real hardship. (It is interesting to note that men of the North Vietnamese regular units also seem to lack this endurance.) Also, as the American soldier's training has done little to prepare him for operating in the difficult Vietnamese terrain, he is at a disadvantage when he moves to seek out and pursue the Viet Cong. Perhaps the biggest weakness of the American combat units in Vietnam, though, is in their use of propaganda and civic action. Most Americans there seem to have only the vaguest idea of how to win the trust and friendship of the people.

Recently, I was discussing my observation of American units and their poor approach to civic action with an American colonel serving in Vietnam's IV Corps area—where there are no U.S. combat units, only U.S. advisors. The colonel conceded that the average American soldier was probably inexperienced in dealing with the Vietnamese, but, he said, "Certainly they're better than our soldiers were in Korea. There they referred to every Korean as a 'gook.'" I was forced to tell the colonel that in many of our combat units "gook" is a term still used when soldiers speak of the people—not only Viet Cong but friendly Vietnamese. I had even heard this term used by enlisted men talking directly to Vietnamese shop owners. The colonel was, of course, disturbed to hear this, but he should not have been surprised. Unless they are taught differently, it is natural for children to act as their fathers did. The American soldiers have not been taught how to behave in Vietnam.

Most of the damage done in the area of public relations is not intentional, but comes about simply because the American is uninformed about the Vietnamese. He doesn't realize the damage certain actions he is likely to perform can cause and he is unaware of the ability of the Viet Cong to capitalize on his mistakes. Two of the most publicized mistakes were made on two successive days in August 1965, in villages near Danang. At Chan Son, several civilians, some in air-raid shelters, were wounded or killed by an American barrage after a Marine unit received sniper fire from the village. At Cam Ne, a large portion of a village from which sniper fire had been received was arbitrarily burned to the ground. There is no question that these actions themselves created a large number of enemies for the United States forces; however, a bigger mistake was to move out before something was done to repair the damage and prove to the villagers that this type of thing is not American policy. Subsequently it was learned that in both instances Viet Cong propagandists were back in the villages as soon as the Americans left, to make sure that a hateful image of the Americans stayed with the people, and at Cam Ne, the Viet Cong brought in a large force to help the villagers rebuild the homes that the Americans had destroyed.

While the Viet Cong were rebuilding in Cam Ne, the Marine commanders in Danang busied themselves with trying to counter the bad publicity they had received from the original operations. They claimed that the houses at Cam Ne were actually Viet Cong bunkers and that it was a military necessity to destroy them. As to the dead villagers of Chan Son, it was said that such casualties are a hazard of any war, particularly a guerrilla war. But while the Americans made excuses in Danang, the Viet Cong were securing their propaganda victories in the villages.

The Marines, however, were not the only ones who failed to see the mistake that had been made nor how fast the Viet Cong would act on such a mistake. All America missed it. Two months after the incidents, an American magazine was still collecting money to rebuild the homes of the Cam Ne villagers—homes that had long since been rebuilt by the Viet Cong—and though Cam Ne is less than five miles from the center of Danang, and presently surrounded by U.S. Marines, it is difficult to control.

While the damage done by such acts is obvious, it can perhaps be written off because of the relative infrequency of such major errors. More important are the actions of United States troops when they are not fighting and have no contact with the enemy. This includes their off-duty hours, their hours in camp, and the time spent on routine operations when no contact is made—probably ninety-nine percent of their time. In all counter-guerrilla operations, whether by Americans or South Vietnamese, a great deal of time must be spent in passing through villages and populated areas. As they search through the villages, the troops may find a few Viet Cong, but they will also find a lot of people who, though often forced by circumstances beyond their control to harbor and help the Viet Cong, do not like the Viet Cong. With such people, the behavior of the American serviceman who comes into contact with them is crucial to our success or failure. The initial reactions of a villager to American troops are the hostility, as to any foreigner, and the fear that he will be harmed or killed. As practically no American servicemen speak Vietnamese, and there is a critical shortage of qualified interpreters, the citizens of a newly entered village are often herded together like cattle and treated as prisoners until the area has been properly searched for weapons and other evidence of the Viet Cong. The villagers are generally released without having been harmed physically, but the psychological damage remains. In the evening, after the Americans have left, the Communist political cadres return and start a discussion about how the "American invaders" treated the people. The Americans may have dragged the village chief through the village at gun point and severely injured his dignity, if not his person. This may be understandable, as a village chief looks like any other Vietnamese to an American soldier, but the Viet

Cong cadre-men can take him and the other offended people aside and with gentle verbal persuasion, not torture, convince them that the next time the Americans come they will probably pull the triggers on their guns. The cadre-men can convince the villagers that they must prepare to defend themselves against the Americans.

"A walk in the sun" is what American troops call the typical fruitless searching operation in which they do not see the Viet Cong all day, but through the terror they create in the villages and their failure to communicate their pacific objectives on these operations, they often leave a few new Viet Cong in their wake.

Of course, the American soldier can't be told not to touch these civilians or to turn his back on any of them. There have been too many "little old ladies" and ten-year-old children throwing grenades to allow this, but a little tact in handling these people might reap surprising gains. For example, if at least one soldier in every squad could be taught a few simple phrases like "would you come with me, please," his unit might be able to make a more favorable impression in the villages it passes through. If the pace of operations could be slowed so that the same units could pass through the same villages more frequently, it would give the troops a chance to get to recognize the people, and give the villagers a chance to understand that the Americans are trying to offer them some measure of defense and do not intend to hurt them. Passing through a village once every three or four months cannot help but do more harm than good unless some massive Viet Cong force is captured in the process.

One encouraging sign is that the Marines at Danang are beginning to understand that they must move slower and secure their rear-guard by effective civic action. But the Marines are leaving the execution of this civic action program to some two hundred poorly equipped and trained Vietnamese and are doing nothing to train Americans to deal with the aspects of civic action that could be carried out without a working knowledge of Vietnamese. In fact, American troops are often forbidden by regulations to do things that if handled properly might produce favorable results. For example, the Vietnamese like to eat C rations, and they also break down cans and weld them together to make metal objects and siding for their homes, but in many areas, troops who have extra C rations are not allowed to give them to the people, and some are even forced to carry the empty C-ration cans back to camp with them. The military logic behind this is sound, in that the commanders reason that the Viet Cong may get their hands on the cans, make bombs out of them, and leave them for some unsuspecting GI. This certainly could happen, but it might be wise to allow individuals on the scene to decide whether the risk is worth taking for the goodwill that might result.

However, this is not the way the military mind works. A commander wants to give an order that will serve in all instances. He does not want his men to think or make decisions if it can be avoided. So instead of telling his men why it might be dangerous to leave C-ration cans lying around and the things that should be considered before doing so, the commander flatly says, "Don't do it." Such a traditional attitude toward giving orders is one of the key problems in the conduct of this war. It makes no real difference whether or not the troops are allowed to give C rations to the villagers, but it does make a difference that they are not encouraged to think and make decisions and are not given the information necessary for them to make decisions effectively. Failing to do this, we lose one of our greatest possible assets—a well-educated soldier who is quick to comprehend the complexities of a situation once they are explained. The Viet Cong, even though they work with uneducated recruits, have done much more than we have to train people to think for themselves. They have done it because their troops often operate in small units with poor communication and must constantly make decisions for themselves. But the reasons for which they have trained their men to think are not important; the benefits they are receiving from the training are what count.

The American soldier, of course, has several strikes against him before he ever sets foot on Vietnamese soil. He is a foreigner, and a non-Asian foreigner at that; and he knows nothing about Vietnamese customs or traditions. He can't speak the language and, whether he realizes it or not, he does most of his communicating with the Vietnamese with the gestures and expressions he uses and with his foreign-sounding voice. It is difficult, but not impossible, for any man to make a favorable impression with these handicaps; on the other hand, it is no problem at all to make an unfavorable impression.

Also, the fact that the complexities of Vietnamese society have not been adequately explained to the average soldier causes him accidentally to create as many problems for his government in his off-duty hours as when he is working. The traditional military attitude toward a soldier on liberty in a combat zone is, "he fights hard and he must play hard." Indiscretions are overlooked because "the troops have to unwind." In so doing, drunken servicemen literally chase Vietnamese girls in the streets, fight with pedicab drivers over fares, and shout abuse at Vietnamese salesmen who try to bargain with them. (In Vietnam, as in many Asian countries, bargaining is the primary way of transacting business. It is not done in an attempt to cheat, but with the idea of both parties arriving at a mutually acceptable price in each sale.) Often when American servicemen are asked what they know is an excessive price for something, they presume that the Asian is trying to cheat them and violent scenes result. In most cases these incidents are passed off as unfortunate, but unimportant. Yet, they are important. There are always Communist propagandists ready to fix in the minds of the average Vietnamese citizens the idea that Americans are an unruly and uncouth bunch of foreign invaders who want to bully and eventually destroy the Vietnamese people.

Military men, as well as some civilians in the U.S., argue that we shouldn't expect our soldiers to be politicians—rather we should expect them to be fighters: "Let the politicians worry about 'winning the hearts and minds of the people,' soldiers are paid to kill!" Some of those who do not believe that the military should be involved in politics go so far as to say that a "good soldier can't be a good politician at the same time." Whatever the merits of these arguments, one must not confuse a narrow concept of politics with the difficult, necessary task of winning the confidence and support of the Vietnamese people. Many American soldiers—both officers and enlisted men—have shown that much can be done to build this respect and friendship without abandoning a solid military presence. More could be accomplished *if* and when every American serviceman in Vietnam is properly trained to make his contribution to both aspects of the struggle.

The American forces in Vietnam must learn to wage political war as well as engage in military actions. Much of the Communists' success comes from their effective use of propaganda and political persuasion among the people, and unless Americans can institute a program of political activism in the field—even down to squad level—the Viet Cong will continue to reap lasting victories despite our military successes. One example of what can be lost through the lack of effective political action is worth citing. A few months after the 173rd Airborne Brigade arrived in Vietnam, it conducted a relatively large operation in War Zone D, northeast of Saigon. It was not a major success, but it did net several Viet Cong casualties, and several tons of rice were captured. As the 173rd's casualties were light and the U.S. claimed a victory, the story was sent around the world by the major wire services and was printed in most of the U.S. newspapers. However, after the Americans withdrew, the Viet Cong directed a propaganda barrage at the peasants in and around War Zone D. The Viet Cong claimed in posters, leaflets and personal contacts that they had killed "one hundred American invaders." The VC also told the peasants that tons of rice had been stolen from the area and sent to the government-controlled town of Bien Hoa, several miles away. (American trucks carried the rice through the starved refugee village of Tan Uyen to the relatively comfortable residents of Bien Hoa.) The Viet Cong claimed that the Americans didn't care about hungry Vietnamese peasants. That the world thinks the operation in Zone D was an American victory, while the people who count, the peasants living in the area, think it was a Viet Cong victory, throws new light on a great discussion that raged throughout Vietnam and the United States in 1965, the topic of which was, "What happened to the Viet Cong Summer Offensive." It may be that the VC were so busy making political hay as a result of the mistakes of the U.S. troops that they didn't have time to conduct military operations, for the Viet Cong believe they can win the war by winning the people to their side and that they can do this without firing a shot as long as the U.S. troops continue to alienate them.

Despite the failure of the American military to develop successful civic action tactics in Vietnam, it can't be said that U.S. troops do nothing of a socially constructive nature. U.S. forces have several projects in which they provide villagers with medical aid, build schools, and supply food for refugees, and there are also individual soldiers who work in orphanages on their days off and who spend a large portion of their pay for such things as sweets for the children. It goes without saying that such activity should not be discouraged, but the projects should be coordinated for maximum effect. When "civic action" is left entirely to individuals acting as the spirit moves them, the result is bound to be spotty. Certain people will get all the benefit and others will get none. Coordination would not prevent individuals from using their own initiative in acts to gain the confidence of the people, but it would help keep civic action aimed at the right objectives.

When the military does get involved in organized civic action it is too often with the idea of gathering intelligence information. One hears of clinics where an interpreter asks every patient if he's seen any Viet Cong recently. While medical aid is not withheld if the patient has no information of value, it doesn't take the peasant long to figure out that the Americans are hoping their medical aid will turn him into an informer. Also, he can't help but draw the conclusion that if insufficient intelligence information is produced, the clinic will probably be taken away. Political activists of the Viet Cong will convince the peasant that every act of the Americans in the village area is of a threatening military nature, and the U. S. troops, untrained and ill-directed in tactics of political warfare, will continue to lose in the real struggle against the Communist forces.

In the Kennedy era, a vast review was undertaken within the military system to try to discover what new techniques were needed to counter Communist insurgencies. A whole new military language was born, but other than this, the general conclusions of the study were that "the book"—much of it written by von Clausewitz in the early 1900's—was sound. It was declared that all the age-old military tactics still worked in this type of war if performed properly. Consequently, nothing has changed much in the methods of training men to be soldiers. They are toughened and trained in conventional methods of warfare, with only a little more training in hand-to-hand combat than before, and sent to fight "the new type of war" in Vietnam. It is true, of course, that to some extent the military men were right, as all the tactics in "the book" have some application in Vietnam. But the degree to which they apply has changed since World War II and Korea, and there is a totally new book—as yet unpublished—on tactics that Americans have never used before, but must use if the war in Vietnam is to be won.

# 2: VIET CONG

Mao Tse-tung listed four golden rules for guerrilla forces: (1) When the enemy advances, retreat; (2) When the enemy halts, harass; (3) When the enemy avoids battle, attack; (4) When the enemy retreats, follow. To this, North Vietnamese Defense Minister Vo Nguyen Giap added six rules of conduct: (1) Take nothing without permission; (2) Never be disorderly; (3) Learn and abide by local customs; (4) Stay with the poor peasants and help them with their work; (5) Make propaganda all the time; (6) Form study groups for the peasants and attend their open meetings. The effectiveness with which these rules are being followed is what is causing the United States forces their trouble in Vietnam.

It is significant that only four of these rules should deal with military tactics, while six concern relations with the people, as most Communist strategists agree that establishing good relations with the people is the most important aspect of guerrilla warfare and the first step to gaining complete control of an area and its inhabitants. The Communists recognize that a government seldom has the physical power to control an entire population against its will for any great length of time, but they have learned that people can be led by propaganda to believe that the best thing for them is what their leaders decide is best. However, in order to control a population in this way, the leaders must be able to control the contacts of the individuals with the outside world, and this is what the Communists are fighting for in South Vietnam.

It is extremely difficult for an American to describe the actions of the Viet Cong or to analyze their effectiveness without the opportunity to live with them and watch them work. Nevertheless, by carefully observing their activities from our side of the fence, we can hope to draw certain valid conclusions. Many years ago Viet Cong cadres quietly moved into remote villages that were at the time of little interest to the government and began their propaganda work. Now the Viet Cong are rapidly moving toward complete control of the peasants in some areas of South Vietnam. As a result of their success, they now operate in areas where the people are friendly to them, and will supply them with protection, food, and intelligence information, at the same time denying this assistance to the South Vietnamese troops. It is natural for the peasants to support the Viet Cong, as many VC have been living in their villages all their lives, or at the very least have been permanent fixtures in the area much longer than any South Vietnamese government forces. The government's propaganda handouts and the brief forays of government propaganda-teams into Viet Cong controlled areas cannot begin to compete with the propaganda circulated by long-time residents of the area. The ever-present Viet Cong capitalize on such popular grievances as high land-rents, poor irrigation facilities, bad wells, and the lack of markets for the peasants' goods. The Viet Cong point out that these are things that a government could, and should, do something about, for before the Viet Cong arrive, many peasants have never thought of the government as an organization existing to do things for the people. The Viet Cong promise that the people will have all the things they need and want as soon as the "corrupt politicians" are thrown out of office and replaced by the leaders of the National Liberation Front, and the Viet Cong show the people how to begin to build a government that tends to their own needs at the hamlet or village level. As this is the first experience the peasants have ever had with a government that seems primarily to have the people's well-being in mind, they think that the Viet Cong are the force that knows how to organize such a government on a national scale. The Viet Cong are also careful to provide extra labor at harvest time, weapons for self-defense, and cadres for education so the people will believe the Communists' promises for the future.

The Viet Cong are cautious not to promise to do things and then fail to produce, and whenever they take something from the people they pay for it, or at least leave a signed receipt. When they first begin work in a village, they always listen carefully to the people, but as they become better acquainted with village conditions, they begin to take control of all activities. Usually some peasants object to the VC taking control, but the peasants learn that they have no power to throw out the VC

**THE AMERICAN SOLDIER**

101st Airborne soldier eats C rations as radio operator contacts other units **(top).** Burning Viet Cong hut **(middle).**

Marines race toward helicopter with poncho full of captured supplies **(bottom).** Ist Cavalry soldier carries captured North Vietnamese **(right).**

Marine suffering from heat exhaustion. Temperatures as high as 130° have been recorded during Marine operations **(top, left).** A typical panji stake trap along a trail uncovered by the Marines during an operation **(middle, left).** A Marine holds a bamboo whip designed to swish across the trail and stab passing soldiers **(bottom, left).** The gate across the trail was booby-trapped with a grenade. The gate was closed and opening it set off the grenade **(bottom).** The Marine **(right)** had his hand shattered opening the gate, and a corpsman works on his hand.

Viet Cong jungle camp with a fire pit in the hut and a bag of rice, horseshoe-shaped for easier carrying, lying near the pit **(top).** American soldier capturing North Vietnamese soldier uses caution against possible grenade trap **(bottom).**

Captured Viet Cong in the Mekong Delta **(top, right)** and captured North Vietnamese PAVN **(bottom, left).** The other two are captured villagers, possibly Viet Cong sympathizers, but probably not gun-carrying Viet Cong.

# THE VIET CONG

American soldier ties the hands of a captured North Vietnamese PAVN **(top, left)**. Viet Cong camp follower admitted to traveling with and entertaining the Viet Cong for over two weeks **(top, right)**. Captured PAVN **(bottom)**.

A suspected Viet Cong receives the water treatment. He is held upside down in a water barrel until he is just about to drown. Then he is pulled out and interrogated. Interrogation such as this is frequently seen when traveling with South Vietnamese military units and often includes beatings with a club and threats with a knife. This man, who was probably an innocent peasant, lived through the interrogation, but produced no information of any value.

South Vietnamese soldiers: in the jungle, eating rice, riding to battle in a helicopter and wounded.

# SOUTH VIETNAMESE ARMY

Dead Viet Cong lies out of his hole as South Vietnamese rangers move on across the rice paddy with prisoners **(left)**.

Twelve-year-old mascot of Vietnamese troops was formerly with the Viet Cong as a message carrier. One day he turned in his Viet Cong comrades to these government soldiers and has since lived and operated with them **(above).** Vietnamese interrogate South Vietnamese villager **(below).**

A popular force soldier (one who fights only in his home district) gets out of a boat after returning from an operation. A destroyed Catholic church is in the background **(left)**. Because of the many streams and canals in the Mekong Delta, where over fifty percent of the South Vietnamese population lives, boats are an indispensable part of every operation. The soldiers fighting in the Delta are half submerged in water most of the time.

A South Vietnamese ranger walks with a young boy whose soldier-father has just been killed by a Viet Cong booby trap.

**THE ADVISORS**

An advisor holds his M79 grenade launcher over his shoulder after a brief skirmish with the Viet Cong **(top left)**. An armor advisor talks on the radio. Many advisors feel that their most important function is to serve as liaison between Vietnamese and American support elements **(top, right)**. An advisor to the popular forces helps carry a wounded soldier **(bottom)**.

An advisor wounded in the back by grenade fragments is helped by another advisor **(top).** An American medical advisor helps a wounded Vietnamese **(bottom).** A Special Forces advisor **(right)** establishes communication with other Special Forces units after a helicopter has dropped his team near the Laos border.

**SPECIAL FORCES**

After a two-week jungle patrol one Special Forces advisor has a beard long enough to comb **(top).** Another Special Forces advisor trains Vietnamese special forces in judo and camouflage at the Special Forces training center **(middle).** An Australian advisor with the Special Forces chews out his interpreter during a jungle patrol **(left).** Special Forces advisors move along a Viet Cong jungle trail near the Laos border during a long-range patrol. This was a main supply route until the Special Forces uncovered it. Then the Viet Cong picked a new trail **(right).**

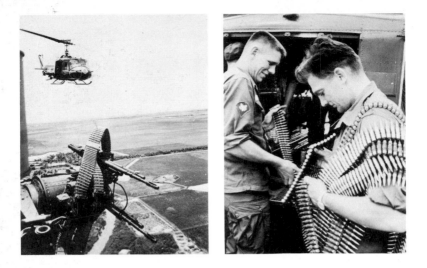

Helicopters armed with machine guns and rockets fly over the Mekong Delta **(top, left)**. Gunners loaded down with machine gun ammunition reload the helicopter's guns **(top, right)**. Troop carrier helicopters land at a rubber plantation for a pickup **(bottom)**. Gunner on a troop carrier helicopter **(right)**.

# HELICOPTERS

American troops race out to helicopters during an operation in South Vietnam. The helicopter has become an indispensable adjunct to nearly all American operations. It is used to lift troops in and out of areas and for medical evacuation and re-supply.

and that the VC punishes dissenters severely. The Viet Cong cadres remain in a village long enough to convince the rest of the peasants that the dissenters are enemies of the people and then the VC are in complete control. (This may sound too simple to be true, but for men as skilled in the uses of propaganda as the VC cadre-men are—who can work with simple people in an area free from outside influence—it is a surprisingly easy task to accomplish.) Finally, when the VC get control, they continue to treat the people with as much respect as the need for discipline allows, for by this they hope to hold the support of the people without resorting to force and in this they usually succeed.

On this subject, Che Guevara, the political theorist behind the Cuban Revolution, says, "Conduct toward the civilian populace should be governed by great respect for their traditions and customs, in order to demonstrate effectively the moral superiority of the guerrilla soldiers over their opponents. Except in special circumstances, there should be no executions without giving the accused person an opportunity to clear himself of the charges." The Viet Cong, who certainly have no qualms about executing dissenters, try to observe this principle and carry out executions only after elaborate public hearings.

Though this is the ideal method of operation, it is obvious that many mistakes are made in its actual implementation. Vietnamese and American officials in Saigon are quick to cite instances where the Viet Cong have terrorized the people and have failed to carry out their stated objectives. The frequent references to these incidents in the press lead the American reader to think that they are so widespread and damaging that they cause the Viet Cong to lose the support of the people, yet there is reason to believe that this is not the case. There have been instances, for example, when the Viet Cong have destroyed buses loaded with civilians or government troops, committing a wanton act of terrorism in the government's view. But government investigators learn from peasants in the area that the bus drivers had forcefully been told by the Viet Cong not to use that road or to carry government soldiers, and whatever the government spokesmen may say, the peasants have been taught to see the destruction of the buses as a natural punishment for disregarding the orders of the Viet Cong.

In our eyes it is murder when the Viet Cong kill South Vietnamese hamlet and district chiefs. However, in the eyes of the Viet Cong these men represent an enemy government and are enemies of the National Liberation Front. As the Viet Cong either live in the hamlets or spend more time in them than the government representatives do, there is no one to counter their explanation to the people that all South Vietnamese government officials are enemies and should be killed. The Viet Cong try not to injure a peasant unless he takes a government position, helps a government official, or in some other way disobeys the laws of the National Liberation Front, and though the peasant may not like these laws, he understands them.

The National Liberation Front has established rules that the peasants know they must obey or suffer punishment, but it is often difficult for the peasants to comprehend the reasons behind the punishments they bear at the hands of government forces. It is difficult for the peasants to understand a sudden air strike on a village or the "harassment and interdiction" fire, which is designed to prevent the Viet Cong from having freedom of movement but which actually kills as many farmers as it does Viet Cong. The peasants see no reasonable way to anticipate these actions or avoid the punishment. As has been said, the Communists' main purpose in fighting in Vietnam is to obtain the right to propagandize among the people. They are convinced they can win the peasants to their side if they can control the information given. They fight to keep the Americans out of the areas they control, as they are afraid the Americans may turn the people against them.

Americans may be convinced that the NLF is not truly a movement for national liberation, but this matters very little. What really counts is what the peasants think of this movement, and many of them believe it is everything the Viet Cong say it is. They have never been given any information that contradicts this impression, and the military tactics of the Viet Cong reflect their determination not to let the peasants hear the other side.

The Viet Cong do not mind the American or government troops roaming through their territory for a few days, as they usually can turn these operations into propaganda victories as soon as the hostile troops retire. The thing that worries the Viet Cong is that the Americans might stay and develop a good propaganda and civic action program of their own. Consequently, when any sizeable American unit moves through one of the Viet Cong base areas, the Communists either try to engage small isolated sections of the American unit, over which they would have unquestioned superiority, or the Viet Cong follow Mao's first law by fading into the jungle and letting the unit pass. If an American unit halts or sets up a base camp, the Viet Cong constantly harass the camp in an attempt to force the commanders to hold a large percentage of their troops in the camp to defend it. The Viet Cong also follow Mao's second law in mounting harassment operations in areas where the people support the government so as to sow seeds of doubt and resentment against the defenders. If a small unit sits in its base or outpost and stops patrolling, the VC will organize an attack to overrun the post. Following Mao's third law, they will do this only if there seems to be no chance of failure. When American and government forces give up battle and start withdrawing to major enclaves, the Viet Cong implement Mao's fourth law and follow the units, harassing them all the way.

This type of warfare is very frustrating for the non-guerrilla soldier. He seldom sees his enemy, and then only in small numbers or for brief periods, but he is always aware that the enemy is near at hand, as his units may receive mortar fire or he may run into booby traps or be shot at by snipers. Wherever he goes he will find firing positions prepared by the Viet Cong, yet he will not make contact with the enemy in the ways his training has led him to expect. Although Americans are adept in the logistics of massive assaults in areas where large units of Viet Cong are thought to be marshalled and can produce lightning-fast retaliation to a Viet Cong attack, these operations seldom net even a small percentage of the original VC force believed to be in the area when the operation is launched. The guerrillas disappear as soon as the government forces begin to arrive unless they are absolutely sure that they can defeat the attackers. If these forces come by foot, the VC are warned by their outposts, and if they come by helicopter, the VC are warned by the artillery pre-strike that precedes every major airlift. The guerrilla force breaks up into small groups and disperses in a number of directions, and the small units can out-maneuver and travel faster than a large force. Also, the Viet Cong are generally much more familiar with the area than the government troops are. They know the trails, the tunnels, and where to find boats. The only situation in which they have difficulty in evading the troops on such large operations is when they are in open terrain where aerial observers can spot them. But even in the vast open spaces of the Mekong Delta there are many wooded areas, particularly along canals, that give the Viet Cong opportunities to evade the forces of the government. Thus, it is almost a maxim that no contact will be made after the first thirty minutes of a large operation unless such contact is made on the terms dictated by the Viet Cong through sniper fire or ambush.

On air lifts, American troops must land in the middle of a Viet Cong unit in order to expect any measure of success, though the Viet Cong still may get away with most of their force. In a recent operation, a small village-defense unit ran into a VC force of undetermined strength. Immediately a heliborne force of a hundred men that was on its way to another operation was diverted and set down only a hundred yards from the heavy weapons of a Viet Cong regiment. (The Viet Cong positions were camouflaged and the helicopter pilots couldn't see until the moment they touched ground exactly what they were getting into.) On landing, though the government troops were out-gunned and out-manned by a force of at least ten to one, the Viet Cong started retreating. This battle was not of the VC commander's choosing. He knew that if he stayed to fight, the Americans would eventually bring in enough forces to defeat his entire regiment. So he moved out, not even stopping long enough to take his heavy weapons. After a bitter and valiant fight, the VC commander lost almost a hundred men, but he saved over nine hundred. By his actions he was observing one of the cardinal rules of a guerrilla: "Fight on your own terms or employ a strategic retreat."

Likewise, the VC likes to plan carefully. Recently, I went with a reaction force that was chasing a Viet Cong unit that on the night before had attacked the Tan Hiep airfield, near My Tho. We went some twenty miles from the field to a place where prisoners had told us we might find the Viet Cong. Although we didn't find many Viet Cong there, we did find bamboo and coconut palm leaves tied together to simulate the shape of an outpost near the airfield. Women in the village told us that the Viet Cong had used this two nights before in a rehearsal of their attack on the outpost. It appears that a Viet Cong commander will often draw up his plans while his troops, their weapons hidden, are widely dispersed, working at regular jobs in fields or villages. He will take lookouts around the target area for many days to make sure he knows the sequence of activities and that it does not vary. He briefs his troops on the plan and may even have a full dress rehearsal before execution. Before the attack, he will lead his troops into the exact positions they will hold just prior to the commencement of firing, and then he pulls them back and gives them a critique. When everyone knows his assignment and all other factors are favorable, the commander brings his troops together and hits the target. If anything goes wrong prior to the attack, he can abort the mission and try again later. Immediately after he completes the mission he disperses his troops again to avoid retaliation.

The Viet Cong military units are not all men. Women and young boys are often used to carry messages, gather intelligence or carry out sabotage. Some women work as nurses and help transport supplies. The Viet Cong also have their own traveling shows similar to those of the USO which have the primary purpose generally of selling a propaganda line, and secondly to improve morale. Women are used in many of these shows. Also, in addition to their armed personnel, the Viet Cong conscript many local citizens to help in transporting their badly needed supplies. This is particularly true in the central highlands, where so many supplies are needed for the North Vietnamese regular units and so few people are available for any type of work, but massive conscripted labor is generally found in all Viet Cong "base areas."

The 173rd Airborne Brigade has spent a good part of the last six months wandering through one of the largest Viet Cong base areas, War Zone "D." Their mission has been to try to make contact with large Viet Cong units and to find the massive stockpiles of supplies that are known to be hidden there. Their tactics have been, for the most part, flawless examples of large conventional operations, and though they have turned up some supplies and killed a number of Viet Cong, they have not hindered the Viet Cong's long-run operations. The reason for their lack of success seems to be simple, in that what they are looking for doesn't exist.

The Viet Cong do not have any fixed installations that cannot be moved quickly or abandoned with ease. In most of War Zone "D," the jungle is so thick that any man, given fifteen minutes' warning, can evade a force of any size, moving out with everything he can carry on his back. Also, it is impossible to see a camp or a supply dump until one is right in the middle of it. By having many small camps and supply dumps, rather than a few big ones, and by letting the jungle hide their positions, the Viet Cong can have many secure bases without using a single soldier to protect them. If the Americans or government troops happen to stumble onto one of them they give it up and write it off as no great loss.

Recently I went on an operation with a Vietnamese Ranger company to a Viet Cong jungle camp they had passed through a few weeks earlier. They suspected that the VC had returned to the camp and they hoped to catch them napping. The Rangers had the exact position of the camp plotted on their maps and all the men had been in the camp before. Nevertheless, it took a hundred men two hours of searching in an area no more than four hundred yards in diameter before one of them finally stumbled into the camp. The Viet Cong themselves often find it necessary to employ guides who have lived in the jungle for many years and know it well in order to get their troops to the base camps.

It seems that the Viet Cong seldom re-occupy one of these camps once they discover that the position has been compromised. It is too easy to build a new camp. Most of the permanent facilities in the camps can be built in a matter of days from materials readily available in the jungle. The living conditions in them are not plush by our standards, but they are perfectly satisfactory by the standards of the Vietnamese peasant.

As the Viet Cong forces grow larger, certain problems arise. They begin to aim at bigger targets that require more men and they find it difficult to assemble their troops without being detected. Also, it seems that the North Vietnamese regular units (Peoples Army Vietnam) are trying to function as regular military units rather than using the tactics of guerrillas. After the action at Plei Me, the PAVN continued to move through the jungles in battalion and regimental formations rather than breaking into small units, as guerrillas might have done so as to evade the aerial observers. General Giap's regular Viet Minh units used such formations when they were fighting the French in the 1950's, and many American commanders in Vietnam expect the Communists, and particularly the PAVN, to continue to form into larger and larger units and begin to fight a more conventional type of war. If this happens, American commanders are convinced that they can defeat the Communists with superior firepower and mobility.

Evidence suggests that Communist strategists believe that they must eventually have this large scale frontal type of action with their enemy despite the fact that neither the victory in China in 1949 nor the victory over the French in Vietnam in 1954 can be attributed to a decisive defeat of the enemy in frontal assault. And though it is true that we have had no battles of anything like the size or intensity of those between the Viet Minh and the French forces, it is assumed that combat with the PAVN will eventually develop on a large scale. It is unlikely, however, that the PAVN units will allow themselves to be defeated as regular soldiers rather than revert to proven guerrilla tactics. And even if the North Vietnamese regulars can be defeated in the field, it doesn't mean that the war will be won right away. There are still thousands of experienced Viet Cong guerrillas to go on fighting, and it would probably take years to subdue them and destroy all their means to resist.

When I first arrived in Vietnam in August 1963, there were less than 20,000 Communist troops in Vietnam. At the end of 1965, it is estimated that there are some two hundred thousand, and more than a hundred and twenty-five thousand of these are operating in guerrilla units. It is my firm belief from observation that most of the latter number will not stop fighting until they have been killed, jailed or their last weapons taken away.

# 3: VIETNAMESE TROOPS

The operations of the American combat units in Vietnam have done more than anything else to prove to me how effective the Vietnamese soldiers are. I had spent almost 18 months in Vietnam before the first United States combat troops arrived, and up to that time I was convinced that American troops could do a much better job of fighting the war than the Vietnamese were doing. The Vietnamese were improving all the time, as they got more and more officers whose jobs depended on their military skills rather than their political affiliations, but there was still a lot of room for improvement and I expected the U.S. combat units to be vastly superior.

Every now and then an American military advisor would tell me, "These are good troops, as good as anything we've got in the U.S." I could never bring myself to believe them, but now I must apologize as United States combat units in Vietnam have proved them right.

I could not believe that American troops would move as slowly as the Vietnamese, yet they move slower. I could not believe that it was impossible to solve the problem of how to keep radio equipment in working condition so that ground units can keep contact with flanking units and with higher headquarters. But the problem remains unsolved, and U.S. troops are having the same trouble with their radio equipment that the Vietnamese have always had.

The Vietnamese soldier is poorly educated, and it usually takes much more time to train him in the use and maintenance of technical equipment than it would take to train an American. Unlike our soldiers, the Vietnamese has been trained from childhood to do only what he is told and not to think for himself, and though individual initiative is not characteristic of the average Vietnamese, this lack often proves to be a military advantage in that a Vietnamese soldier will almost never question an order by his commander no matter how suicidal the mission may be. On the other hand, if communications break down during an ambush or the commander of a unit is killed, the Vietnamese soldier is at a loss as to what to do as there is no one to give him orders, and even lieutenants and non-commissioned officers are often unwilling to make decisions in a pinch. As Vietnamese soldiers need much more direct supervision than Americans, the degree to which they operate effectively is much more dependent on the abilities of their higher field commanders, and the direct orders given, than it is in the U.S. Army.

Two of the most outstanding units that I have ever operated with are the 42nd and 44th Vietnamese Ranger Battalions, both based in the Mekong Delta. These units are made up of hand-picked troops who are absolutely fearless in battle, and they are well trained and have excellent commanders. I place them well above any American unit now stationed in Vietnam for skill and efficiency at fighting the Viet Cong. The fact that I have singled out these two examples does not mean they are the only good Vietnamese units. There are others I have observed that are almost equal in quality to the 42nd and 44th and I am sure there are a number of other units that are also very good.

In the less elite units there is a great problem in that the Vietnamese generally—and thank God this includes the Viet Cong—are notoriously bad shots. This is due partially to the fact that it is difficult for these small men to handle large, high-powered weapons, but probably more important is the fact that they have had very little training before they are sent to the field. (The North Vietnamese regulars, who have more formal training, seem to be doing better.) The Vietnamese also have poor fire discipline, and one round of sniper fire will often prompt them to fire several magazines of ammunition without ever seeing the target. Their operations at night consist mostly of manning outposts a few hundred yards from their camps and in setting ambushes, but too often the outpost and ambush positions end up in the same spot night after night. Consequently, it is easy for the Viet Cong to locate these positions and to overrun them at will.

The troops are poorly paid and the housing for their families, who often accompany them, is often below the peasants' standards. As they are not made aware of the importance of maintaining good relations with the peasants, they "appropriate" rice, chickens, ducks, and all types of food to supplement their rations, and this, of course, does not endear the soldiers to the people. On the other hand, we should not blame them too much, as American soldiers "appropriate" knives, pictures, drums and other souvenir items from the villagers. In fact, the biggest single advantage over the Americans that the Vietnamese have is that in living closer to the peasants they understand their problems and know their hopes and fears.

The combat experience of the Vietnamese troops is invaluable. Not only do they gain this from their three-year obligated military service, but if they are young men, they have spent their entire lives in a country at war. Many in the Home Guard, or Regional Forces, have served in the regular army before taking their present jobs, and the experienced Vietnamese soldier can distinguish the Viet Cong from the peasants better than an American soldier will ever be able to.

Despite the newspaper reports that make it seem as if Americans are the only ones fighting in Vietnam, there is still one very large and important area where only Vietnamese are operating —the Mekong Delta. A vast area stretching from the north near Saigon down to the southernmost tip of the country, the Mekong Delta is designated for military purposes as the IV Corps area. Major General Dang Van Quang, one of the ablest leaders in the Vietnamese military, is the Corps commander. With more than six million of South Vietnam's sixteen million people living in the area, and with its productive farmland, it is the country's most valuable asset, and excepting the capital itself, it is the most important area, militarily and politically, in all of Vietnam.

There are American advisors and U.S. support troops, such as helicopter crews, based in IV Corps, but no U.S. ground combat units, nor is there likely to be in the near future. It is rumored that General Quang has told his superiors that he does not want U.S. combat units in his area. Evidently he feels that in spite of the weaknesses of his own Vietnamese troops, it would be disastrous to bring any of the U.S. troops now in Vietnam into the Delta. Such troops would cause more social problems in this densely populated area than they could possibly solve.

In defense of the American combat units, military spokesmen point out that they have only been in Vietnam for nine months, and should be given time to get experience before they are criticized. But I'm not so sure. Most American soldiers will serve a year in Vietnam and then leave never to return. They will be replaced by green troops with no combat experince who will have to start at the beginning in learning how to fight in Vietnam, and the American officers are slow to learn that their concepts of military tactics must be adjusted drastically when they arrive in Vietnam.

Over the past two years I can remember many instances of American officers criticizing the Vietnamese for undertaking massive operations that produced little or nothing in the way of Viet Cong casualties. Very seldom were such tactics praised, yet the American combat troops are now in Vietnam and their commanders are mounting the exact same sort of operations. Except for improvements in tabulating Viet Cong casualties so as to make the Americans appear to be doing better than they are, most of the tactics employed remain the same.

One of the primary strategies now proposed by the American commanders is to set up bases of operation and slowly expand their perimeters, clearing the terrain of Viet Cong as they go. Then Vietnamese civic action teams are supposed to come behind the American troops and perform the necessary civic action to win the people to our side and set up an effective government. Many of the American commanders are presenting this as a new idea, but the Vietnamese troops have been using it since the fall of Diem.

As the Vietnamese have learned, the original clearing operation usually works well, but too often the pacification projects break down after the civic action teams go to work. In most of the projects there are too few teams, the members lack experience and training, they often are not adequately or efficiently supplied, and they are given impossible time limitations to work under. In many cases they have barely begun when the military commander, reluctant to leave his troops overlong in one position, prematurely expands the operation. With the troops gone, the VC soon slip back into the villages where they assassinate the officials and everything is right back where it started, and there is every evidence that the Americans will make the same mistakes as the Vietnamese.

To give an idea of the time required for a successful pacification project, evidence to date suggests that the United States Marines who are now starting such a project around Danang Air Base will need two years to establish any sort of effective government in the villages located just within a ten-mile perimeter of the base. The Marines now have two thirds of a division tied up at this task, and unless the units become more effective than they are now, the number employed cannot be reduced without severely hurting the program.

To tie up so many troops in pacification efforts may seem to be a big waste, but the Viet Cong can easily destroy all the work that has been done if they get back into the hamlet before the officials have had time to establish themselves firmly and before propaganda cadres have had time to indoctrinate the peasants. Also, it takes time for the benefits of American economic assistance to be felt by the peasants, and though the program might snowball if it ever got started, there is little hope for this if the officials, particularly the Americans, are not patient enough to give it the time it needs to work. Whatever the future of these projects, the Vietnamese should not be blamed for having used the wrong tactics in the past, as the Americans are finding now that they must operate in the same way.

# 4: THE MILITARY ADVISOR

> "How can we lose when we're so sincere."
>
> —Charlie Brown. In a Peanuts cartoon seen pasted on the locker door of a U.S. advisor in the Mekong Delta.

A year or so ago an American captain who had just arrived in Vietnam reported in to the Vietnamese captain who was commanding officer of the battalion the American was to advise. The Vietnamese opened the conversation by saying, "They've sent you to advise me. I've been fighting the Communists in this province for more than ten years. I've been commanding officer of this battalion for more than four years. For the first six months I'll advise you; then maybe you can advise me." To an officer who had never had any combat experience this made sense, and by the end of the year they had both learned a great deal. I heard this story second-hand and it may not be true, as Vietnamese are seldom this outspoken, though many of them certainly feel this way when they are assigned American advisors. Still, if it is true, it probably led to a successful association.

In reviewing what I've seen in two years of watching advisors come and go, it is obvious to me that the program has been quite successful. Washington, prior to the arrival of the first U.S. combat troops in 1965, tended to identify all American personnel in Vietnam as "advisors," but in truth the term should be reserved to designate the men who actually serve in the field with the Vietnamese units. These men are at the lowest levels of our advisory chain of command, and they are in the closest and most constant contact with the average Vietnamese. As the battalion advisor's job is almost entirely military, while the sub-sector advisor's job is probably three quarters social-political, the latter will be discussed in another chapter.

In all of South Vietnam there are approximately one hundred and thirty government battalions, and though the official strength of the units is set at about four hundred and fifty men —slightly more in Airborne and Marine battalions—at times, such as the end of 1964, their strength may fall to as few as two hundred and fifty men. Each Vietnamese battalion is authorized three American advisors—two officers and one senior enlisted man—and this means that there are almost four hundred men serving in this function on any given day in Vietnam.

The senior battalion advisor, usually a captain, is assisted by a first lieutenant. The NCO, whose primary job in theory is to train enlisted men in the use of their weapons, in fact generally functions as a radio-man on operations and, like the lieutenant, provides an extra set of eyes to spot faults. Their observations are passed on to the senior advisor, who in turn makes recommendations to the battalion commander, through whom most suggestions are channeled.

Many people see the military advisor as someone standing beside a unit commander checking every move he makes and saying, "Yes, I agree," or "No, you shouldn't do that," but this is not the way it is done. In the heat of battle, the commander can't be bothered with some advisor telling him what to do, and there is certainly no time to discuss or argue about decisions. More important, once a battalion commander has made a decision, he must insure that it is carried out; otherwise he loses his authority and the respect of his troops. If he seems in doubt, and waits always for the American to tell him what to do, his troops will soon know who is really in command. If an American tried to act this way, he would only undermine the man he is trying to help. Consequently, there is very little advice given during actual operations. As one advisor put it, "I do my best advising over a beer after the operation is over." It is best for him to pick out something he saw during the day that could have been done better or differently and discuss this with the battalion commander in the relaxed atmosphere of a restaurant, away from the eyes of the troops. Perhaps after discussing the problem the commander will act differently in a future situation. The method is slow, but in the long run effective.

One advisor who felt that his suggestions were being ignored once complained to me, "I'm nothing but a glorified communicator." And, to watch the advisors during operations, this often appears to be the only thing they are doing. They serve as ground coordinators between American aerial observers, American helicopter pilots and occasionally American Air Force fighter pilots. If the Vietnamese back in higher headquarters are procrastinating or making decisions that the battalion commander thinks are incorrect, he will often have his advisor call back and support his decision through the American chain of command with the hope that the senior American officers can put a little pressure on his own superiors. This sometimes works, though often the efforts of both the Vietnamese commander and the American advisor are frustrated.

Another important function of an American advisor is that of playing supply sergeant. The Vietnamese supply system frequently grinds to a halt in red tape, and while the American system isn't so much better, the battalion advisor can generally get needed items faster than the Vietnamese can. In example, the basic weapon of the Vietnamese army is the American carbine. Though most of these carbines are built as semi-automatic weapons, there is now a conversion kit that can turn them into automatic weapons. These kits are in short supply and the Vietnamese battalion commander doesn't even try to order them through his normal supply channels. When he wants them, he tells his advisor and the advisor goes through American channels to get them. The American sometimes has problems, of course, but he will always get the kits much faster through his supply system than the Vietnamese can through his.

When an advisor's tour is finished, he is often convinced that his most important accomplishments in Vietnam were in helping his assigned unit function better with the American helicopters and air power, and in getting his unit the supplies it needed. He knows that the combat experience he gained will be of value to him as a career officer, but he often feels that his advice has not done much to improve his unit's methods of operation.

My conclusion though is that the military advisors do have an effect. It is difficult to explain how or why it happened, but Vietnamese units that have the enemy cornered, and just about boxed in, no longer stop for lunch in the middle of battle; they're more aggressive than they used to be; they're more conscious of proper security; and there are fewer incompetent officers. I like to give the battalion advisors and those sessions over a bottle of beer a lot of credit for the improvements.

Perhaps it is the right time for me to make a confession. When I arrived in Vietnam I was one of those confirmed civilians who have served their time in the military—four years as an enlisted man in the U.S. Navy—and who were convinced that the only people who made careers in the military were those who couldn't make it on the outside. I felt that career men were looking for the soft life of the peacetime military, in which all that's needed to make a steady salary is to keep one's boots polished and stay out of trouble. I thought the professional soldier hadn't the drive or the ambition to get ahead in the business world, but these young advisors have proved me wrong. They are certainly among the best men the U.S. has to offer. They have the intelligence, drive, and ambition that make outstanding leaders in any field. They are military men because they prefer that service to business and industry, though I am convinced that most of them would be successful in any field they chose to enter. This praise, however, does not extend to all American officers in Vietnam. With a few notable exceptions, I have found it to be the rule that the higher the rank of the officer the less he understands about Vietnam's problems and how they should be combated. The longer these officers have been in the Army, the more they tend to rely on what they have learned from past wars, and this seems to be leading them astray.

The younger men, the battalion advisors, do not make command decisions and are only supposed to carry out orders. They do this with skill, intelligence, and ingenuity, but at times if they sense, through their close association with the people and the troops in the field, that the orders they are given are wrong for this war, at this time, they are still in no position to change them. They make recommendations, but these have not seemed to bring about any change in overall tactics.

One reason they seldom press for changes in overall tactics is that good officers trust their superiors to know more about fighting wars than they do. One often hears an advisor say, "I don't know much about the overall war situation as all I see is the little isolated area I work in," but these little isolated areas are the same all over Vietnam. Though the terrain and the people may differ somewhat, the basic problems are the same.

In theory, the advisors at the lowest levels report their findings to their superiors and the superiors look at the big picture and issue orders to solve the problems. In actual fact it doesn't work that way. Mountains of paperwork from the provinces must be sent to Saigon each week in order to answer the thousands of questions that those on top want answered, but the problem is that too many of the questions are those that may have needed answering in past wars but are not necessarily applicable to this one. And though the junior officers are not likely to argue with their superiors on questions of policy, they have had the most intimate contact with this "new kind of war" and probably know more about it than the senior officers with years of military experience.

The American commander, General Westmoreland, spends many hours of each week traveling about the country talking to the men in the field in an effort to gain their perspective, but it must be extremely difficult to obtain the same insight that a battalion advisor has acquired in living closely with the Vietnamese. This understanding is very difficult to communicate, especially if a young captain is talking to a man wearing four stars, and though I am not suggesting that General Westmoreland or any other senior military men are not doing their best to comprehend the problems in Vietnam, I only want to emphasize how difficult the problems are and to show why the optimism often voiced by our senior military officers may be misplaced.

I am convinced that the war in Vietnam will never be won with the tactics we are now using, but to expect these tactics to be changed is something akin to expecting the chairman of the board of a corporation to accept from a junior executive the advice to change completely the company's approach to its particular business, to do away with the jobs of several vice-presidents, and to put the junior executive, and others like him, in charge of running the corporation. It is highly unlikely that such a thing would happen in the American business world and it is even more unlikely that it will happen in the U.S. military.

The tactics that may be necessary to win in Vietnam have never been tested, nor even fully outlined, and the American command seems to be reluctant to try anything that has not been fully proved in past wars. Since Korea there have been only two basic modifications in our tactics—increased use of special forces and helicopters.

# 5: SPECIAL FORCES

Many Americans think of the Special Forces as a semi-secret counter-guerrilla force which harasses and sabotages the enemy behind his lines, but there is nothing secret about the operations of the Special Forces in Vietnam, where their primary job is to recruit and train civilians for Civilian Irregular Defense Groups, or CIDG. The members of the CIDG, who function primarily as a defensive force, are paid better wages than the regular Vietnamese soldiers, and they always live near their homes and may leave the employ of the Special Forces whenever they desire.

In preparation for recruiting these civilians, the Special Forces sets up Forward Operational Bases, or FOB's, manned by a small group of American and Vietnamese cadre-men and a few defensive troops. The FOB's are generally established in the center of an area that has been controlled by the Viet Cong for some time, and are often on a supply route used by the VC and usually near a large village. Once the Special Forces group, or "A" team, gets a foothold, it begins to work, through propaganda and civic action, to convince the people that it has come to stay, that it will defend the people and improve their standards of living, and that the people should do something to defend themselves. Then as local men volunteer, the Special Forces brings them into the FOB compound, trains them and builds up a fortified camp. In most cases, such a camp will eventually have between four hundred and five hundred CIDG recruits from the area, and will be commanded by a dozen each of American and Vietnamese Special Forces cadre-men. There is nothing clandestine or covert about the operation, and from the moment the camp is established the Viet Cong know exactly where it is located and subject it to constant harassment. In nearly every case the FOB's are established in areas where the Viet Cong have had free access and complete control for years and in this sense they are behind enemy lines. After their establishment, the Viet Cong still has free access to most of the area, the FOB serving only as an island of government control in the center of Viet Cong territory. As the Viet Cong can control the roads, if in fact there are any roads, these islands must usually be supplied from the air.

A secondary mission of the Special Forces, and one that at present is being de-emphasized in favor of other operations, is border surveillance, but there has been no real attempt to seal the borders, as no one from Special Forces has ever thought it possible. At the moment there are some sixty Special Forces FOB's, with approximately eight hundred U.S. advisors and twenty-eight thousand CIDG, near the seven-hundred-and-fifty mile border that separates Vietnam from Laos and Cambodia, but as the terrain is covered with dense jungle, most FOB commanders find it difficult to maintain regular patrols any farther than three or four miles from their camps. While they occasionally have patrols that reach much farther, these are not frequent enough to hamper Viet Cong movements or to even give an accurate indication of what the movements are. Because of the difficulties of patrolling the jungle, almost none of the FOB camps are close enough to each other to have interlocking areas of responsibility, so it is easy for the Viet Cong to continue to move between any two camps without being discovered. This is particularly true along the northernmost section of the border that separates South Vietnam from Laos, where there are only two Special Forces camps.

Because of the isolation and relative ineffectiveness of such camps, it is argued by some that the FOB's should be established in the coastal valleys where the population is greater and observation is easier, but at present, the Special Forces have no camps in the lowlands paralleling this section of the border.

When the Special Forces decide to set up a camp in a new area they look first for a pattern of Viet Cong activity and then try to locate the camp in the middle of it. From the moment the Special Forces begin to set up a camp, the Viet Cong usually concede that the area has been taken from them, and while the Special Forces are settling in, the Viet Cong begin to set up a new series of supply trails that will avoid the camp. By the time the Special Forces has its CIDG completely trained and ready to operate, the VC is using an entirely different area for the movement of supplies and troops. Given the present number of camps, the VC seem to find it wiser just to keep the Special Forces penned up in the camps rather than expend the large forces necessary to take and eliminate them. In most cases the Special Forces maintain the camps once they are set up rather than trying to relocate them frequently, and in the past two years more than half the FOB's have remained where they were established, and the rest have moved, on the average, only once.

In the spring of 1965, several augmented Special Forces "A" teams were given the additional mission of serving as sub-sector advisors in their districts, and in six of the border provinces, Special Forces men serve at the sector level as advisors to the province chiefs. These assignments were made to bring about a smoother coordination of all activities within the districts, and to take full advantage of the intensive training every Special Forces soldier receives in conducting basic social welfare programs.

These three tasks—training soldiers, border surveillance and advising the district chiefs—are the responsibility of the Special Forces in Vietnam. In the training of soldiers they serve much the same task as the battalion advisors, but they feel they can do a better job because they have bigger teams and because they control all their own supplies. Even the pay of the CIDG troops comes through the American "A" team commander, thus avoiding any problems that might arise from the Vietnamese handling the money.

The operations of the CIDG are very similar to those conducted by regular Vietnamese battalions, except that the CIDG may run a few more patrols to gain intelligence information than the regular battalions. American Special Forces soldiers argue that the CIDG conduct more frequent and better patrols than the regular government troops, but my experience with both types of units indicates that they both have the same faults. Regarding any Vietnamese troops on patrol in territory that is firmly held by the Viet Cong, a Special Forces officer once said, "The Vietnamese (Special Forces soldiers) and the CIDG think a patrol is a hundred men. Maybe the first ten and the last ten are militarily necessary." (And he seemed to have some reservations about it being necessary to have even 20 men on such a patrol.) "But the other eighty are just along to make noise." This opinion reflects a favorite theory of many Americans in Vietnam that the Vietnamese soldiers move slowly and make plenty of noise while on operations in order to alert the Viet Cong that they are in the area and give the VC time to get out of the way, but in the time I have been observing them, both the CIDG and the regular army units have improved greatly and most of them are faster and quieter when moving through jungle than American units of similar size. Still, there are very few patrols conducted by anyone in Vietnam that could be considered clandestine.

The duty in an FOB is often considered more dangerous than that of other troops in Vietnam, as the camps are so isolated and have no heavy-fire support other than air power. On the other hand, these camps are so heavily defended from the inside that while they are often harassed, they are seldom penetrated, and only once has a camp been completely overrun. In this one case a large number of Viet Cong had inadvertently been recruited into the CIDG—a constant problem that is impossible to solve completely—and one night the infiltrators started an attack inside the camp. Fortunately, though, the command group was able to evacuate the camp, reorganize their forces and retake it.

While the Special Forces are proud of their ability to defend the FOB's, they try to play down the importance of the camps as permanent bases, and emphasize instead their patrolling and intelligence-gathering activities, but to have these bases is to be forced to defend them, and ten Viet Cong with a mortar tube can force the FOB commander to employ almost half his men in the defense of the base at all times. This defense is vital, as in every base there are large quantities of the food, weapons, ammunition, medical supplies, and tools needed to support the five hundred military men and the civic action programs the Special Forces undertake. It is necessary to cache these items in large quantities because of the difficulty of getting anything to the camp, and the danger that it may have to hold out for long periods under attack without replenishment of supplies. It is certainly not desired that the VC get their hands on such a stock of equipment, and if someone starts shooting mortar rounds at the camp, there is no way of telling if it is just ten men or a battalion of VC waiting for an opportunity to overrun the camp. This ability of the Viet Cong to keep the men cooped up in the bases, coupled with the difficulties of moving through the dense terrain that surrounds them, limits seriously the intelligence information that can be gathered by the FOB units.

In order to do something about closing the intelligence gap, one other project was started within the Special Forces around the end of 1964. Known as "Project Delta," it was kept highly secret until the end of 1965. The Project Delta units, or "D" teams, are made up of Americans and Vietnamese, with a maximum of ten men to a team. Sometimes as few as three members of a team will go on a patrol, but they are not meant to engage the enemy and are used exclusively for intelligence-gathering purposes. Though most of their patrols are now run from two to five days, the units are designed to undertake patrolling operations lasting as long as fifteen days. The "D" teams may use one of the FOB's as a base or they may operate out of some higher headquarters, but they are highly mobile and require very little in the way of support. At the moment there are only a few of these teams, but in the light of a number of major intelligence coups on which regular units were able to capitalize, there is likelihood that the number of "D" teams will be increased in the near future. Still, at present the contribution of these "D" teams is only a minute part of the entire Special Forces effort in Vietnam, and they are the only units that can be said to be operating covertly near the enemy without his being aware of them.

There are those who suggest that the Special Forces are doing many things of great importance in Vietnam that are kept secret, and though this is possible, I seriously doubt it. First of all, there just aren't that many men trained in Special Forces tactics, and the number of men in training would have to be greatly increased before more could be put into the field. Another thing is that the trend of Special Forces activities seems to be away from highly skilled jungle fighting, and toward activities similar to those of all other advisors in Vietnam. Thirdly, the Special Forces concept seems to be losing the support and favor that it had a few years ago with senior commanders.

Presently, Special Forces activity is directed toward recruiting and training soldiers overtly in enemy territory in South Vietnam and it seems unlikely to me that any covert bases have been set up in North Vietnam as there is still so much more that needs to be done in the South. Also, it would be next to impossible for Americans to operate in the North, as the North Vietnamese have firm political control over every village in their territory, and to supply an American team in the North would pose very difficult logistical problems.

If any Special Forces teams are being sent into North Vietnam for purely intelligence purposes it seems that they would almost certainly be Vietnamese, as anyone who didn't look Vietnamese would almost certainly be picked up by the police the moment he was noticed. Early in 1965 the Vietnamese government announced that they had sent several members of their Special Forces into North Vietnam on various occasions, and though they did not give any indication of the total number of men involved, they did admit that almost eighty-five percent were captured before they could even begin their missions. Too, if there are intelligence or sabotage teams operating in the North, the results of some of their exploits would probably come to light, just as the first information on Project Delta appeared. In late 1965, the operations of the "D" teams led to a series of victories, and as it was felt that the value of publicizing the victories outweighed the desirability of keeping the methods of operation secret, the news of the victories and information regarding the "D" teams were released. For these reasons, I believe it is safe to assume at the present time that the classified or unreported aspects of the Special Forces operation in the Vietnam war are not significant in the overall effort.

VIETNAM IN THE MUD

# 6: HELICOPTERS

It is an axiom of war that the man with the greatest mobility wins, or at least has a tremendous advantage over his opponent, and mobility in warfare is usually interpreted as the fastest way to get soldiers from one point to another. If one adheres to this simple definition and if one considers improved mobility the key to winning wars, then the wide-scale use of helicopters to transport troops would seem highly advantageous. However, two questions ought to be answered before one automatically assumes that "helicopter warfare" is a good idea: (1) How much increase in mobility is there really? (2) What is lost, if anything, when helicopters are used to increase mobility?

The helicopter takes the soldier to the point where he begins his operation faster than he could get there by any other means, but once on the ground, the soldier is just as much a foot soldier as his opposite number in the Viet Cong. Unlike the VC, though, an airlifted unit begins a ground operation with its position and strength already revealed by the maneuvering helicopters, and, flying in from a base many miles away, the troops are unfamiliar with the terrain. American commanders believe that their units can cover much more territory than the Viet Cong through the use of helicopters, and U.S. soldiers are constantly flying from one spot to another. However, as this mobility doesn't allow them time to become familiar with the people or the terrain in which they are operating, the Americans usually fail to convince the villagers that the operations are undertaken for their protection. Furthermore, as the training of American troops is based almost entirely on the use of helicopters for movement and support, they are not prepared to live off the land and are unable to operate without almost daily re-supply from the air.

The helicopters themselves are not infallible, and keeping them in the air requires extensive maintenance, which, in turn, ties them to fixed bases. They are very vulnerable to enemy gunfire and the pilots often find it difficult, if not impossible, to land in an area where the Viet Cong are located, and if an operation takes a helicopter away from its regular base for any length of time, fuel supply becomes a major problem. Such are only a few of the reasons why helicopter warfare is somewhat impractical, but perhaps it is better to explain the problems by relating how helicopters are actually used on operations.

A few months ago I was in the Mekong Delta looking for a battle to photograph when I discovered that a routine helicopter operation was being planned by IV Corps headquarters. Intelligence had indicated that five hundred Viet Cong were massed in a certain area, and the officers planning the operation calculated that it would take five battalions of Vietnamese troops, or about two thousand men, to block the five apparent exit routes that led from the area, and during the operation, armed helicopters were to maneuver over the rice paddies to prevent the Viet Cong from cutting across the open fields. The possible paths of exit were either tree-lined canals or other wooded areas that the Viet Cong could use without being spotted from the air, and all of these exits had to be blocked on the ground in order to seal up the VC concentration.

However, the problem of getting each battalion to its position was complicated by the fact that there were only twenty helicopters available, and as each can only transport ten men, it would be necessary for the entire formation to make two trips to each position. The entire airlift would require ten forty-minute round-trip flights, with stops for refueling every other trip, to transport the five battalions.

According to the operation plan, the first troops were due to land in the target area at about 8:00 in the morning; however, as the intelligence information indicating the Viet Cong position was eight hours old and the force might have moved in the interim, it was necessary to "prepare" the landing zone with artillery and air strikes so that the first wave of two hundred men wouldn't land in the middle of the entire Viet Cong force.

Now to look at the operation from the Viet Cong side: It is 7:30 and the VC are cooking their morning rice when the first artillery rounds begin to land. Immediately the Viet Cong move away from the area of the artillery strikes, and the commander begins to disperse his troops as widely as possible with the intention of regrouping after the action is over. The VC commander prepares to fight a delaying action with a small number of men so that the major element of his force can get away. He would consider fighting a major holding-action only if he occupied an impenetrable position, and such is not the case.

By the time the Viet Cong have begun to disperse, the commander sees that the artillery rounds are concentrated on several points in the area, and as he knows that the strikes are directed at what are believed to be Viet Cong positions, if he can only move between these points he will be safe. Following this strategy, he heads his troops for the nearest exit, using as many routes as possible so that his force will not be bunched together in a large group. He does not consider making a stand, only how to escape.

The routes along which the Viet Cong will travel are the densely wooded strips that line the canals in the Mekong Delta. The land for fifty feet on either side of the canals is covered with heavy foliage under which the farmers build their villages. Movement of troops under the trees is very difficult to spot from the air unless the men are concentrated in large groups and as long as they remain dispersed they can move fairly freely.

Now it is 8:15. The first helicopters have yet to land, but the VC commander has had forty-five minutes to move his men away from the pre-strike area. By this time, the VC are pretty well organized. They know where the center of attack is going to be, and they know that the government will try to surround the area as quickly as possible. Though they don't know the direction from which the first government troops will come, they can be sure that the landing will be somewhere within the pre-strike areas. In five minutes they will know.

At 8:20, the first helicopter-flight lands with approximately two hundred troops. As the helicopters cannot land in the treeline along the canal, they land in the nearby rice paddies and the troops hit the ground, where the real trouble begins. The helicopters have done all they can for them by dropping them five hundred meters from the treeline, but now they are simply infantrymen like the Viet Cong. The troops prepare to move into the trees, but they must wait about fifteen minutes for a ten-man squad to go ahead and check to see that the unit isn't walking into a trap. Once in the treeline they take up positions along the canal and wait for the helicopters to come back with the rest of their unit before moving out.

Some may ask why they don't move out right away. But they may be still facing a Viet Cong force of as many as five hundred men and they must be strong enough to fight. So they wait. At 9:30, two hours after the Viet Cong commander learned there was to be an action against him, the first battalion is assembled and ready to move out. The helicopters now have to refuel.

By 10:30, troops will be blocking another route of exit, but it will be afternoon before all the exit routes are secured, and though the helicopters have transported nearly two thousand men fairly quickly over twenty miles of difficult terrain, the Viet Cong are hours ahead of them and know exactly what the government troops are up to. By late afternoon, when the battalions are reassembling to be lifted back to their bases, the Viet Cong have moved out of the area without a single casualty.

From this operation in the Mekong Delta, one should not get the idea that the limited loads they can carry and the noise they make are the only drawbacks to using helicopters in Vietnam. There are many more. For instance, just one bullet in the right place can knock a helicopter out of commission, and Viet Cong sharpshooters know the place and are getting better at hitting it. Because of their vulnerability even to small-arms fire, helicopters must land in tight formations and as quickly as possible so as to give the Viet Cong little time in which to aim or correct their fire. In order to maintain these formations, they must have a relatively clear approach to the landing area and must commit themselves to it long before they touch the ground. All of this negates the really unique qualities of helicopters, in that they cannot hover, or land, as should be possible, on almost any spot of flat terrain.

I have never seen a transport helicopter hover during a combat assault operation, and to land, they swoop down from about fifteen hundred feet, touch ground long enough for the troops to jump out, and get back up to fifteen hundred feet as fast as they can. It is the only way to keep them flying for another operation. They are vulnerable and their pilots know it.

When the 1st Cavalry Division was sent to Vietnam, most American newspapers carried pictures showing how the 1st Cav's helicopters were going to land on steel nets on top of the jungle, but those pictures were taken in the United States, not in Vietnam. Such a maneuver requires a helicopter to hover low over the jungle while dropping or picking up troops, and in Vietnam, if there are any Viet Cong in the area, any hovering helicopter will almost certainly be shot down. On the other hand, if there are no Viet Cong in the area there is no need to put troops on top of the jungle instead of using a nearby jungle clearing. Such a tactic might be useful in evacuating a wounded man from the jungle, presuming it were possible to get him from the jungle floor to the tree tops where the steel net is laid, but from what I've seen of the Vietnam jungles it would be much easier and faster to carry the wounded man to a clearing even if it took days to get him there.

The important question about this tactic is not so much whether it will ever be used in Vietnam, but how it ever got into the operational handbook in the first place. The man who thought this one up had no concept of what war in Vietnam is like, and yet valuable time has been wasted in teaching helicopter pilots and troops how to perform the maneuver.

Another new tactic developed by the 1st Cavalry Division is that of dropping men into the jungle by rope-slide from a hovering helicopter, and again, some of the same problems arise. The helicopter must hover while the troops slide down the ropes and it must come in slowly in order to assume a hover position. If the Viet Cong are right under the helicopter they can shoot it down, and if they have heard the helicopter coming and have cleared out of the vicinity, the American troops sliding down the ropes will probably never catch them in Vietnam's dense jungles.

There were only five exit routes in the Delta operation, but there are hundreds in the jungle. One can pass thirty feet from an enemy and never see him. When troops are landed in the jungle by helicopter, everyone for miles around knows where they are, and it has been my observation that troops landed by helicopter in a jungle area haven't got a chance of finding the VC unless the VC wants to be found. Though it is true that one can point to successes we've had in the jungle as a result of using helicopters, no one but the Viet Cong can say how many of these successes were due to our good luck or to poor VC leadership. Similarly, only the Viet Cong know how many times our large search units have passed near a Viet Cong force without spotting it. However, it seems dangerous to rely on a tactic that can only work if the enemy has tremendously bad luck or poor leadership, and no one can deny that a Viet Cong force has a tremendous advantage in evading a relatively large American unit whose exact position is frequently pinpointed by re-supply helicopters.

Helicopters are useful when things go according to plan, but the Viet Cong don't play by the rules set by those who plan helicopter operations. In the fall of 1965, I photographed part of an operation with the 101st Airborne in which a unit was dropped by helicopters into a clearing near the base of a range of jungle-covered mountains. According to the plan, the unit was to set up a blocking force at the foot of the range and intercept a Viet Cong force that was being pushed in their direction by another Airborne unit coming over the mountains. There was no real reason to expect the VC to retreat in a straight line into the trap, rather than move in one of a dozen other directions, but this was the plan.

In any case, the Viet Cong, as usual, were not where the Americans thought they were, and the first elements of the blocking force were set down only fifty yards from a VC regimental command post. At the outset, three helicopters were shot down and every other helicopter was hit. This happened at 8:00 in the morning and because of the intensity of fire in the area, only a couple of helicopters were able to land in the area during the rest of the day.

Despite the lack of support, the Airborne fought well, and though they took several casualties before they were relieved, they killed a lot of Viet Cong. However, the important thing to note about the operation is that reinforcements could not be brought in by air according to the plan, and it was the following morning before the first relief troops came overland across the mountains. Medical evacuation helicopters could not even get in until the second day.

Another tactic that is gaining much favor is the almost suicidal night combat assault. I've heard a lot of experienced helicopter pilots talk about these operations and the mildest analysis I've heard is, "I think we should have this capability in case of a real emergency, but I don't think we should use it as a routine tactic."

The problem is that most of the men who think up these various operations are not pilots and they generally outrank the senior helicopter pilot in the area. As the operations are being plotted the commanding officer of the helicopter unit will explain that it is very difficult to see where one is landing at night and if the helicopter is set down on the dike of a rice paddy, it will probably turn over. He'll explain that helicopters are perfect targets at night and that it is impossible for armed helicopters to make the usual reconnaissance runs at night, and there is no way of knowing if the Viet Cong are in the landing area until they start firing and by that time it is too late. The helicopter commander may also question how effective the troops will be on the ground at night once they get there. The VC will know the troops are in the area from the sound of the helicopters and move under cover of darkness to set up ambushes. If the troops are going to do nothing until daylight but sit where the helicopters put them then he will ask why they can't be dropped in daylight when the odds of keeping everyone alive are much improved. The helicopter commander will present his arguments and then assure his boss that if it is really necessary, his men can do it. Too often, their courage and skill is abused in needlessly risky operations.

Somehow, it's difficult to convince a senior officer who can't fly, and who has never been in a helicopter when it's getting shot full of holes on a combat assault mission, that helicopters are not tanks. I've often thought that any officer who is to have a part in dispatching helicopters might be required to spend one week as a door gunner on an armed helicopter before he is allowed to endanger the life of any helicopter crewman. If this were done, I feel there would be fewer impractical uses of helicopters in Vietnam. Still, it is difficult to get any senior officer into an armed helicopter, as most of them realize it is probably the most dangerous spot in Vietnam.

An armed helicopter is a UH-1B (Huey) mounted with an assortment of rockets, machine guns and grenade launchers. It is used at altitudes between fifty and three hundred feet to reconnoitre a target area or to support friendly troops on the ground. When searching an area for Viet Cong, the crew often gets its first warning of an enemy position on the ground when the bullets start cracking around the helicopter. Every day the men who operate these aircraft stake their lives that the Viet Cong are not very good shots. As the VC can seldom be spotted from the air unless one of them shoots at an aircraft or unless ground troops are forcing them to move quickly and expose their position, one of the principal services of the armed helicopter is to bait the VC—give them a target they cannot afford to pass up—and then, the minute they show their position, pour lead on top of them. It is an extremely dangerous business, but a highly successful one in terms of restricting VC movement and protecting the unarmed transport helicopters.

The armed helicopter is in some ways the most effective aerial offensive weapon we have for this type of war. It is slow enough and maneuverable enough for the crews to distinguish between an armed Viet Cong soldier and a friendly villager and try to hit the enemy without hurting the innocent. This is not to say that the armed helicopter crewman is always this accurate, as armed helicopter strikes have killed a lot of innocent villagers and will continue to do so, as will almost every man involved in fighting this war. It does mean, however, that the armed helicopter has the potential to be this accurate, as has no other aerial weapon in our arsenal. The only time when the others can be sure of hitting the hostile and not the friendly is when there is nothing but Viet Cong spread over a wide area—a situation that almost never exists in Vietnam.

Whenever I go to do a story on a helicopter unit, the pilots will invariably say, "Don't forget to give the med-evac boys credit." These men have saved a lot of lives and I can assure you they're a welcome sight when you need them. On an operation in October 1964, my platoon encountered some Viet Cong in a village and I was shot in the leg. There was no one with a radio near me and I had to crawl to the edge of the treeline before I spotted a man with a radio who could signal that I had been shot. Three minutes after the radioman had put out the call, a helicopter with a big red cross on its side was sitting there ready to take me aboard. Shooting was still going on a hundred yards away, but the med-evac pilots seldom worry about the situation on the ground. All they need to know is that there is someone down there who needs to be evacuated. It would take another book to relate the risks these crews have taken to pick up wounded men. The Viet Cong will shoot at a med-evac helicopter just as fast as they will shoot at any other, but this doesn't stop the med-evac pilot.

Med-evac pilots deserve a lot of credit, but so does every man who crews a helicopter in Vietnam. Most of these men will leave Vietnam after a year with over a thousand hours in the air and almost every minute of that time they have run the risk of being shot down. Though some areas are safer than others, there is no really safe place to fly a helicopter in Vietnam.

Despite the courage of the crews, helicopters are being misused in Vietnam. These highly mobile craft might be of great value if we were still fighting World War II and needed quickly to bring troops up to a weak point in a stationary front where battle was engaged with an entrenched enemy. But in Vietnam, the enemy breaks contact as soon as he knows that reinforcements are on the way, and in most cases it is the sight or sound of helicopters that informs him. Most of our present tactics are designed to defeat the Viet Cong in major battle, with helicopters as the chosen method of transport, but we find that against the Viet Cong guerrillas the tactics don't work. Still, it is not the execution of the tactics that can be criticized—this is done with as much skill, courage, and dedication as is humanly possible—but the tactics themselves and those who are determined that they be used.

# 7: EQUIPMENT

Despite the operational weaknesses of the helicopter that have been observed in Vietnam, it is the one piece of equipment our advanced technology has produced that can perform a truly useful function in the war. Other equipment, such as armor (tanks, amtracks, and armored personnel carriers) and air power (the fighter and bomber aircraft), has proved to have little practical use and is being overemphasized and overused. The use of such equipment can have no overall positive effect on the war effort, and though the continued overuse of this equipment leads us away from victory and toward defeat, there is evidence that in spite of all the disadvantages, heavy reliance on such equipment is likely to continue.

To begin with, the amtrack and the M113 armored personnel carrier, both of which are amphibious vehicles, lightly armed, and used primarily for carrying troops, have about the same advantages and disadvantages and can be discussed together. The amtrack, which is used by Marine units, is designed to move troops quickly with a degree of protection, and as it is heavy enough to knock down small trees and is able to float, it seems at first glance to be ideal for operations in Vietnam. However, when the heavy amtrack moves into a rice paddy, problems arise. It can move through a paddy only if there is enough water to float it on if the base is firm enough for it to get traction. Unfortunately, when the paddies are flooded, they are very soggy and the amtracks either get stuck, or must take devious routes to avoid them. The M113 is better in rice paddies than the amtrack, but it has trouble crossing rivers and canals. Although it has no problem in floating, it has difficulty in getting out of canals, as most canal banks in Vietnam consist of very slick mud in which it is almost impossible to get traction. Also, when one looks at the construction of the drainage canals in Vietnam, one feels that the builders knew that one day armored personnel carriers would be used against them. These canals are just a bit too wide for the M113 to jump, yet if it tries to cross by going into the canal, it will invariably get its nose stuck in the opposite bank. Consequently, every canal must be bridged before crossing.

In recent months I have been on six operations that used amtracks or M113's. On two of these the amtracks ran out of fuel and the operations had to stop to defend the equipment. On two others, the men of the forward element, though on foot, had to stop and wait for the amtracks to catch up with them. Only in the remaining two operations were they used wisely, in one to convoy a load of troops up a river, and in the other, to ferry troops across a deep channel to a target area.

The element of surprise is always lost when these mechanical monsters are used, as they can be heard from miles away. But more regrettable than their ineffectiveness is the damage done to peasant property on every operation. Although the men who operate the vehicles are aware of the problem and take no pleasure in destroying the peasants' crops, it is impossible to move one of these vehicles through a field without decimating it, and quite a few rice paddies can be crossed in the course of a day's operation.

In theory the peasants are paid for damage to their property, but in order to receive payment they must submit claims to their provincial chief, who may be difficult to find, and even then it can take eight months to a year for the claims to be paid. In the meantime, after our forces leave, the Viet Cong return to the villages and say, "The officials in Saigon do not want to help you. They send men to destroy your rice."

The psychological effects on the peasants of such incidents are difficult to determine, but it is wise to note that the Viet Cong send men to help them at planting and harvest time while it often seems that all the government sends are machines to destroy the crops. This may seem like a pretty shallow reason for supporting the Viet Cong, but we are dealing with simple men whose lives center around their crops and for whom the balance between hunger and making ends meet is a very thin line.

As for tanks, there is almost no terrain in Vietnam that is suitable for their use, yet American units have attempted to use them in the areas around Danang and Saigon—both rice paddy regions. At Danang, though a tank can move on the sand close to the coast, or along the roads, this restricts their movement too much for them to be effective. Around Saigon it is difficult to find any place where they can leave the roads. In both areas it takes tanks much too long to get to an operation area, and once they do arrive they are too restricted in their movement to be effective. Despite their obvious failings, the tanks and amtracks have been sent to Vietnam, and though there isn't much use for them, they still must be defended twenty-four hours a day.

It has been estimated that at any one time, a third of all the American combat troops in Vietnam are engaged in more or less static defense of our bases and equipment. The Viet Cong, on the other hand, have been able to avoid this defensive problem by learning how to live off the land and by not encumbering themselves with unnecessarily large pieces of equipment or with support facilities that they cannot afford to lose. Whenever an American newspaper reports that government forces have destroyed a Viet Cong base area, one should know that this means they have destroyed a few thatched huts and several dirt bunkers, which can be rebuilt in a couple of days. If the VC lose one of their bases, they haven't really lost much, as their equipment is made up almost entirely of things they can carry with them when they move, and if the VC must retreat in haste they still can cache a thousand rifles in fifty small holes and be pretty sure most of them will not be discovered before they return. A tank, of course, will not fit in a small hole, and the only way to defend it is to put a comparatively large number of troops around it.

Defending their equipment, and the bases where it is assembled, probably takes more of the American troops' time than any other task. At Danang there are six combat battalions of U.S. Marines, along with all their support elements, and at any given time a goodly percentage of the "grunts," or Marine infantrymen, must be on guard to defend the mountains of equipment gathered in the area, and in the An Khe valley, an Army combat division devotes a third of its forces to purely defensive operations. Despite this obvious waste of manpower, the trend is not to become less reliant of such facilities, but instead to make the bases more permanent, with many of the comforts of home, and thus more necessary to defend.

Actually, in regard to the overemphasis of the value of equipment, I am not so concerned with tanks and amtracks as I am with all the thousands of small consumable items that our forces find so necessary and without which the VC seem to be able to flourish. Even such obvious necessities as food and water are being provided in ways that cause needless waste of manpower. An example is the attempt to provide American soldiers with purified water even when they are in the field, which means that many cans of water must be trucked or airlifted to troops who often have access to wells and who are always surrounded by fresh water in the canals and rivers. Some American soldiers are told never to fill their canteens from Vietnamese wells or streams unless it is absolutely impossible to get purified water, though a couple of purification tablets can make the well or river water as safe as the purified variety 999 times out of a thousand. In addition to the wasted effort of moving the water and the fact that American units must be so dependent on re-supply, every man has an added burden in that he must carry the extra weight of several canteens.

Food is also a problem, in that the C Ration, while very wholesome and rather tasty once one gets used to it, is probably the least economical food in the world to transport in quantity, largely because it is canned as an individual meal and packed in such a way that the soldier usually throws half of it away. Despite this waste, the local food is seldom used, nor are soldiers encouraged to supplement C Rations with their own purchases locally, and in many areas they are prohibited from eating any local food. The Marines based around Danang are under orders not to eat in the city's restaurants because none of them meet acceptable U.S. military standards of cleanliness; still, the Army advisors who were based there before the Marines arrived not only ate in Danang restaurants, but ate all the same foods their Vietnamese colleagues were eating while on operations. This food would never have met United States public health standards for cleanliness, but I do not know of any advisors who died from eating it. In fact, all advisors to Vietnamese units still eat the local food and almost none carry C Rations or any other type of American ration. If American combat troops were encouraged to buy food locally, it would help improve relations between the troops and local merchants, help support the local economy, release some men for combat who are now tied to logistical duties, and help solve some of our mammoth supply problems. Such a policy would not only be economical and more practical militarily, but would also be appreciated by most soldiers, who get good and tired of C Rations.

Basically, we need to break away from the idea of establishing "Little Americas" in certain isolated spots in Vietnam and instead to teach our soldiers how to live off the local economy as much as possible. The lives of the soldiers might be more spartan, particularly those of the headquarters soldiers, but by forming closer associations with the Vietnamese people, our combat troops might be able to do a better and faster job of winning the war. And that, after all, is the primary purpose for our being in Vietnam.

One argument for these super-bases, or "Little Americas," is that sizeable concentrations of force are necessary to defend our Air Force installations, but in my opinion the U.S. Air Force commitment in South Vietnam is one that could and should be vastly reduced. The Air Force's most valuable contribution to the war effort is the L-19 single-engine reconnaissance plane. With it, pilots can provide intelligence information that can be used by both ground troops and Air Force fighters, but the L-19's do not have the glamour of jet fighters and most pilots do not like to be assigned to fly them. Cargo transport, mostly in multi-engine C-123's and C-130's, is another extremely important Air Force job, as large quantities of supplies must be moved by air, but again is usually considered undesirable duty as it is an unexciting type of flying. However, reconnaissance and cargo transport are only a small part of the total U.S. Air Force operation in Vietnam, most of which is built around the use of fighters and bombers.

The daring bombing and strafing missions the Air Force undertake in Vietnam are heralded as vital contributions to the war, but it can be argued that eighty percent of such missions are doing more harm than good. The enemy targets that are available in South Vietnam are nothing like the factories, supply dumps, railroads and bridges that our bombers so effectively destroyed in World War II and Korea. Viet Cong supplies are widely disbursed in small quantities and their storage areas are almost always impossible to spot from the air. The Viet Cong "factories" of which one hears consist simply of small hand-operated lathes used for manufacturing crude weapons, or a couple of sewing machines for making uniforms, and are located inside thatched huts that look like any other peasant huts from the air. As to any roads, railroads or bridges, they are more valuable to us than to the VC and we try to keep them intact as long as possible.

The only real targets are people, but even the slowest bombers are too fast and too inaccurate ever to be sure of hitting the enemy and missing the friendly. There have been a few instances where large groups of Viet Cong have congregated in an area away from the villagers and decided to fight, and in such cases, if government troops are not too close to the target, bombing strikes can be effective, but such targets seldom present themselves and even then air power is no foolproof means to victory.

One example of effective air strike support and what bombing can do against a concentrated enemy force was given at Plei Me. The quick and continued reaction by U.S. bombers to Plei Me's call for help was probably the only thing that prevented the Communists from overrunning and completely destroying the FOB. It is certain that a large number of enemy troops were killed in the bombing raids, and as the planes were up against a heavily armed and well entrenched force, their speed did enable them to complete their missions with less damage to their aircraft than would have been possible if armed helicopters had been used. Still, after eight days of continuous pounding of the Communist positions, the bombers received automatic-weapon fire on every run.

The battle at Plei Me was an ideal situation for Air Force bombing. The enemy was in a fixed position that he was trying to hold and there were no friendly villagers nearby. All friendly elements were assembled inside the Plei Me Special Forces camp and anyone outside the perimeter was an enemy. But such conditions are rare, and Air Force pilots with whom I have talked estimate that on over eighty percent of the missions they fly neither of these two criteria is met. In most operations air power is used to "soften up" an area prior to putting troops on the ground, in raids on "free strike zones" where it has been decided that everyone living in the zones is a Viet Cong sympathizer, or on areas from which aircraft have received ground fire.

Though "softening up" an area is considered a necessary tactic wherever troops are to be moved in, without doubt there are more innocent villagers hurt or killed in the raids than Viet Cong. If American planes raid a treeline, under which the Vietnamese villages are built, the chances are that any Viet Cong would have been in their fox holes during the bombing. The VC have fox holes dug and waiting in almost every village in Vietnam, and it is necessary for a bomber to score a direct hit on one of the holes to kill a man inside. If anyone is hurt in one of these "softening up" attacks it will surely be a villager.

Recently, I paid a visit to a provincial hospital in the Mekong Delta where I ran across two rather interesting stories concerning bombing. One lady in the hospital had received a nasty napalm burn on her arm, and when she arrived at the hospital, the doctor, a young American, tried to find out when and where she had received the burn. At this the woman was indignant, as she reasoned that being an American, the doctor should know where the bombs were being dropped. This doctor gets many patients with napalm burns or wounds from bombing, as this is a province where the VC are very active, and all the people who come in with burns or wounds know that the Americans are dropping the bombs. The Viet Cong have made sure of that.

In the same hospital there was a boy about 10 years old with a broken leg. About three months earlier his mother had brought him to the hospital after he was hit by bomb fragments. The doctor set the leg and started to put it in a cast, but the mother would not allow the cast, as she said she expected her village to be bombed again and she was afraid her son would not be able to move fast enough with his leg in a cast to get into the bomb shelter. Though she took him home, she finally returned with him after three months as the leg was not healing properly. The doctor asked why she did not leave her village if she knew it was going to be bombed, and she told him she could not afford to leave her land as it was the only way she could support her family.

"Free strike zones" are areas in which everyone is supposed to be a Viet Cong soldier or a VC sympathizer. Unfortunately, many of the people thought to be sympathizers stay in the Viet Cong areas for the same reason as the woman above—because they cannot afford to leave what little land they own. Sometimes the government drops leaflets in these areas telling the people to leave and they will be cared for and given money for relocation, but most of the people who do leave the areas find that it often takes the government a long time to distribute the promised funds and word of this filters back to those who remained. As a result, the Vietnamese we eventually hope to win to our side by proving that our way of doing things is better than the Communist way, are the ones who are receiving the brunt of the bombing, and all the while the VC are quietly explaining to them that the National Liberation Front is interested in the individual, that it goes to the people and tries to discover and solve their personal problems. The Viet Cong ask, "How can you support the American imperialists? All you see of them is their bombs."

Every day hundreds of L-19's fly low-level patrols over South Vietnam looking for Viet Cong movement, and every day some of these planes are fired upon—sometimes by a large force and sometimes by just one or two guerrillas. If a flight of bombers or fighters is available at the time of the incident, the L-19 will direct them to the target where a raid will be made. Frequently, very little is known about the target area other than some fire was received from it, and quite often the target is a village. There are no statistics available on how many people—VC or innocent peasants—are hit by these bombing attacks. Calculations by anyone are pure conjecture.

The type of questionable bombing raids I have been discussing are made by the A-1E's, B-57's, F-100's and F-105's, but the most ridiculous use of air power to date in Vietnam are the strikes of the B-52 super-bombers. These operations are like trying to hit a fly with a baseball bat. The B-52 crews never even see their target. They drop their bombs on a pre-arranged target according to an electronic signal, and though the military planners know that all the bombs from one plane will land in a particular square mile of terrain, they cannot hope for much more accuracy than this. If the B-52's destroy anything important it is pure luck, and any helicopter armed with a load of rockets can do just as much effective damage as is usually accomplished on one of the B-52 raids.

Around the end of 1965 I had a chance to go with ground forces and observe the results of a B-52 bombing raid in a jungle area near the Michelin Rubber Plantation. This was an unusual opportunity as there is seldom any follow-up on the ground after a B-52 raid, but our party got to the area only fifty minutes after the bombs were dropped. In this particular instance a sizeable patch of jungle had been bombed, but we could find no indication that any Viet Cong had ever been in the area. Though the bombs cut several rather straight paths through the jungle, they did not destroy all the jungle along any of the paths. If a bomb landed in rather thick jungle it leveled nothing more than the immediate area around the bomb crater.

Of the craters, there seemed to be two sizes, some about seven feet deep and fifteen feet in diameter and others about fifteen feet deep and thirty feet across. I presume that the smaller craters were made by five-hundred-pound bombs and the larger ones by seven hundred and fifty or thousand pounders. Frequently, the jungle came up to within five or six feet of the craters, and though there were some areas of jungle that appeared to have been opened up considerably, it was obvious from the size and frequency of the craters that these areas had been pretty much cleared before the bombing strike. The bombs seemed to have landed in clusters of two or three, cutting a hole in the jungle. Then we would have to tramp through another fifty or hundred yards of jungle before we could find another clearing. Where the jungle was especially thick, we couldn't see from one cluster of bomb craters to the next.

After we had walked through most of the bombed area, we turned at right angles to the bomb line and started checking the surrounding terrain. After about two hours we stumbled across an abandoned Viet Cong camp only three hundred yards from the bomb line. It consisted of five rather large huts, all separated from each other, though connected by trails, and all completely covered with jungle foliage so they could not be observed from the air. There were rather large quantities of clothing and food in the huts, but none of it had been damaged by the bombing. It would have been pure luck if they had been hit. It would also have been possible, judging from the way the bomb craters were located, for one of the huts to be destroyed while the others were left standing. This is what Americans are getting for the five hundred million that will have been spent simply on B-52 raids in the fiscal year ending in June 1966.

After these observations, I can't help but think that a half billion dollars is too much to spend for an operation that seems to be so completely ineffective, and particularly if the same results could be achieved for a fraction of the figure. If one took the same number of men that are now crewing Guam-based B-52's and let them wander through the jungle for a year, burning and destroying any structures they find, they would do more real damage to the Viet Cong than the B-52 strikes will ever do.

It seems that the factors of cost and effectiveness have never been important in this argument, only that the Strategic Air Command (SAC) has felt it had to prove that it had a place in counter-guerrilla warfare. I am sure that the first B-52 strikes in June 1965 were the result of years of lobbying by SAC commanders in the back halls of the Pentagon, and not because anyone really believed that B-52's could be of value in Vietnam.

The deciding factor was that SAC wanted to prove it could do something other than stand guard for a nuclear attack.

The competition between the four services and their particular branches for funds and continued prestige is much more of a factor in such decision-making than is the question of cost to the taxpayer or the possible effectiveness of the operation. The military establishment knows that in wartime it never has any trouble getting money as it can always claim that American boys will die if the funds are not forthcoming, and though there is no question that it is safer to ride in a B-52 than to walk on the ground in Vietnam, if the B-52's accomplish nothing and the ground troops have to go in and do the job anyway, is it really worth five hundred million dollars a year? Though some may claim that the areas the B-52's are hitting are too strongly fortified for any ground soldiers ever to penetrate and damage, I don't believe there is any area in Vietnam to which a well-trained American Special Forces unit could not travel and do more damage than the B-52's. There may be some that would require artillery or air strikes, but how much more effective the air strikes would be if there were someone on the ground correcting fire and if the aircraft were maneuverable enough to take advantage of the corrections. It would be interesting to ask how many Special Forces units can be trained, equipped and kept operating for a year on half a billion dollars.

In this war, one of the most important considerations for all career military men is to justify their existence and to prove that the jobs they do are important and necessary to counter-guerrilla warfare. They must prove it now, in Vietnam, as "This is the only war we've got." If the Congress, which watches over appropriations, becomes aware of areas of obsolescence in the military, allocations may be cut, and officers in the reduced branches will be transferred to other jobs, for which they may have no training or interest, with the result that their careers may be affected adversely.

The uninitiated may think there are only four branches of the military—Army, Air Force, Navy and Marines—but this is not the whole story. For example, the Army alone has five combat arms—Infantry, Artillery, Armor, Engineers and Signal—in addition to many technical services, and when a career officer joins the service he selects one of these combat arms and sticks with it throughout his career. Each is very specialized, and if a man switches branches his advancement is usually hindered as he first has to acquire the proper background for the new job.

After the Korean War, the number of people in each one of these branches was stabilized on a percentage basis, according to the military requirements of a Korea-type war. But the Vietnam war came along and immediately the Infantry's star began to rise while Armor's fell. Armor, of course, doesn't want to lose any of its funds or manpower, so it tries to prove that there are certain jobs in Vietnam it can do. The Armor commanders argue their case in high places, using reams of statistics, of which enough have been collected in Vietnam to prove or disprove any point one wants to make. Infantry would like to have the extra funds the change in requirements seems to allow, but the Army chiefs reason that Armor served us pretty well in the last war, and we might need them in the next, so we'd better let them work in Vietnam.

Still the competition between Infantry and Armor is nothing compared to the big fight between the Army and the Air Force. The Air Force is determined to prove that its jets are of value, not only in nuclear delivery capabilities, but in fighting the guerrilla bands that are likely to be our major military headache for many years to come. If the Air Force fails in this task, there is bound to be a phasing down of tactical fighter and bomber aircraft, and for SAC it might be the last dying gasp. Ten years ago SAC was the brightest star in our military establishment. It was the organization to join, as in it one had the most exciting and demanding job in the peacetime military. It had a future, or so everyone thought, but then the missiles came and the numbers of SAC aircraft and SAC bases were cut back, and the men who had staked their careers on SAC were losing their chances for promotion.

Despite the seeming obsolescence of the B-52's, the SAC

officer struggles to convince the military commanders that his aircraft still has a tactical value, and though there is talk of closing SAC down by the end of 1970, if a man is cornered he can fight very hard. In this way, there may be more men cornered in the Pentagon than are cornered in Vietnam, and they use every trick in the book to prove they are needed and important.

Though Infantry, for the moment, has the upper hand and is really directing the show in Vietnam, its commanders have tended not to object to the involvement of Armor and the Air Force in the war. Though Infantry presses for greater funds and manpower, there is an element of fraternity throughout the entire military establishment, and no one service or branch ever knows when they may need the support of another in the halls of Congress. Basically, they have all agreed to share the opportunity to display their abilities in the struggle to save South Vietnam.

I am sure that the military men responsible for this sort of bargaining are convinced that what they are doing could not possibly do any harm to their country, and I do not for a minute question the loyalty of any of our military men or their resolution to give their lives, if need be, to protect and defend our country and our way of life. Instead, I think that certain military men, and many civilians in government as well, have made some grave errors in judgment based on past situations and that these decisions should be reviewed at once and corrected where necessary.

# 8: SAIGON AND THE MOTIVATIONS OF THE ELITE

Most of Vietnam's leadership group—politicians, bureaucrats, and businessmen—live and work in Saigon, and their interests and motivations differ widely from those of the peasant masses in the countryside. This elite can see evidences of the war every day, but somehow the reasons for the war and the gravity of the situation never seem to reach Saigon.

The Saigonese see the large numbers of military men who work and relax in the city and the military convoys that move through the streets. Jet planes constantly fly overhead, and small battles occur on the edge of the city almost every night. Often the sky at night is lit by flares over a battle zone, but Saigon residents have lived with this sort of thing for so long that such an incident is of no greater interest than a Fourth of July fireworks display would be in the U.S. The occasional terrorist bombings within the city are only minor harassments, most of which go completely unnoticed by the average Saigon resident. They do remember the terrorist activities of 1953 and 1954, but the 1965 explosions were nothing in comparison to the ones at the end of the French period.

For most of this elite, the war is only a minor upset to their normal routine, and is bringing them economic well-being. The attitude of the elite toward the problems of the peasants, or for that matter the day laborer in Saigon, is much the same as was the attitude of the American people, for so many years, to the problems of the Negro population in the Southern United States. The members of the elite have almost no interest in their fellowman but only in personal power and wealth.

One of the best informed Vietnamese correspondents in Saigon recently told me that the leaders of the various pressure groups have finally realized that they all have one unifying interest—to defeat the Viet Cong—and that this overshadows all differences. Thus, my friend believes, the elite will contribute to no major coups or political shakeups in the foreseeable future. This appraisal may seem a bit too optimistic, but it is true that at the end of 1965 there was little political activity in Saigon.

Certainly, many of the more important political leaders realize that their idealistic fervor of 1964 almost brought about the destruction of South Vietnam in January-February 1965. After the fall of Diem, these politicians felt that if they did not get total acceptance of their wishes immediately, another dictator would take power. Their wishes were varied and conflicting and the bickering and succession of regimes that followed Diem's fall almost completely destroyed the fabric of government and led the common man to give up hope. The politicians may have finally realized that Vietnam is not strong enough at present to stand the shock of their radical ideas and as a matter of expediency it is necessary to work together until their country and government are free from outside interference. Still, these men lack any basic sense of compromise—a fault they may have picked up from the French—and to this they add an exaggerated Asian sense of pride.

The fact that the Saigon politicians have been lying low is no guarantee that there is not a great deal of political maneuvering going on beneath the surface. Vietnamese politicians prefer maximum secrecy in all dealings to any type of open forum, and the first that anyone is likely to know of a new government is when it announces that it has assumed power.

Vietnamese politics is not at all like politics in the United States. The Vietnamese politicians dare not speak openly, for even if they support the current government, there is no guarantee that government will be in power for long. Thus, it is considered the gravest of mistakes to bring political maneuvering into the open before one is prepared to present a "fait accompli." As it is so easy to make a mistake and be on the wrong side at the time of a coup, the favored tactic is never to do anything in public that might tie you to one of the major political movements. For the same reasons, officials in the bureaucracy prefer not to make any decisions for which they must accept responsibility. If the leadership changes, then these officials cannot be blamed by the new government for having made incorrect decisions.

The primary preoccupation in Saigon at the moment, and one that may have distracted the political leaders, is the millions of U.S. dollars that are flowing into the country through direct aid, increased Vietnamese employment by the American military, and well-paid GI's. Most of the people who would have been active in politics before are now spending their time trying to get their hands on as much of this money as possible.

Recently, there have been indications that securing a government job may no longer be the simplest or best way for one to get his hands on this money. Though payoffs are still made on almost every business transaction, these payoffs are much smaller and are going to a much larger group of people than in the time of Diem. Small businessmen can now make a reasonable profit even after making a payoff to someone in the bureaucracy, and Prime Minister Ky and other top-level officials seem to be honest and are successfully curbing large payoffs. The days are gone when a single family could have its fingers in every major transaction in the country.

However, in spite of improvements, bureaucratic positions are still sought, irrespective of the low salaries, as they continue to put a man in a position to take some under-the-table profits. There are still petty bureaucrats who can legally earn only a few hundred dollars a year driving around in Mercedes or other fancy cars. The Vietnamese have become so accustomed to this system that they can hardly conceive of being able to do business without it.

In business, the use of false bills continues as a standard operating procedure. For example, a merchant in the provinces may come to Saigon to buy lumber, a commodity for which the central government has set a maximum price of five hundred piasters per square meter. The lumber dealer in Saigon may charge a thousand piasters per square meter, but he will make out a bill for five hundred. The merchant from the provinces will accept this without a second thought and return home with his lumber, for which he in turn will charge a higher price, yet still hand over a bill that lists the price at five hundred piasters. Though this is certainly a black market operation, it is presently the only way to do business in Vietnam. As well, these merchants probably are not making profits as great as they appear to be in that much of what they are charging above the government standard goes into payoffs.

The payoff system is so ingrained in Vietnamese life that the people usually cannot conceive of paying for anything at the legal rate. An American businessman in Saigon recently hired an English-speaking Vietnamese to take care of paying his income tax for him. The Vietnamese knew that he would be paid well for the job, and the American was reasonably sure the Vietnamese would not try to cheat him. Nevertheless, a few days later the Vietnamese returned with a receipt for two thousand piasters and told the American, "I got you special low rate, but we have to give my friend in tax office ten thousand piasters as a present." But while twelve thousand piasters was a reasonable tax by United States standards, the American knew that Vietnamese taxes are low—usually running considerably less than the five percent maximum—and, considering his income, he thought the sum was a bit too high. Figuring it out himself, he saw that he was legally required to pay something in the neighborhood of forty-five hundred piasters. He showed this to the Vietnamese, who puzzled over it for quite some time before returning to the tax office to retrieve the balance of the American's money. It seems that neither the intermediary nor his contact in the bureauracy had bothered to figure out what the American would legally have to pay in taxes. After all, no Vietnamese does it that way. A taxpayer and a tax collector simply set the lowest figure that the bureaucrat thinks he can slip past *his* boss, and then they bargain over the fee the bureaucrat gets for taking the risk of breaking the law.

Most of the worst corruption lies with middle-level bureaucrats, but they are also the only people in the country at present with the knowledge and experience to run the governmental machinery. If they were to be purged there would be no one left to run the country. Also, if they thought it necessary, a league of these minor officials could organize a force to overthrow the government. It is this dilemma that faces every Vietnamese Prime Minister no matter how honest he may be personally.

With widespread education and a steady improvement in the legal system most of this corruption could eventually be wiped out, but this is not going to happen next month or next year. It can only happen when the rapid military and economic buildup that is now taking place is no longer necessary, and when a government has had time to stabilize and strengthen itself.

The problem of law enforcement in Vietnam, and particularly in the cities, at times seems almost insurmountable. Perhaps the all-time low was reached in August 1964 when bands of unruly teenagers moved almost undeterred throughout the city. At that time, lines of students rolled back police barricades without even slowing down, and it will be a long time before the Saigon police forget the humiliation of those days.

One of the saddest pictures in Saigon is a Vietnamese policeman trying to direct rush-hour traffic. Try as he might, very few people pay any attention to his frantic hand signals, and instead the drivers go blithely in whichever way they please, and whenever they please. Though the result of this behavior is generally massive traffic jams that often tie up streets for hours, the Vietnamese seem to be happier with the present chaos than the order they could have if they all obeyed a few basic laws and showed some respect for one another. The Vietnamese always prefer to express their individuality, even if doing so makes life less convenient for them. They also feel that to accept the authority of someone else is to be inferior to that person. Everything becomes a matter of pride, and a man of the middle class cannot even accept the authority of a policeman without the sense of losing status, and he would rather ignore a policeman's hand signal—and argue for two hours that he has a right to ignore the signal—than to admit that the policeman was correct in stopping him in the first place.

Everyone has heard of the Oriental sense of family, which is as strong in Vietnam as in other parts of Asia, but this is where all sense of community ends. Every individual feels that he has definite responsibilities to each member of his own family, and absolutely no responsibilities to anyone else in the country. They think freedom means the right to do anything they want, possibly short of murder, without having their actions questioned. They do not understand that if man is to have the benefits of society, he must accept certain responsibilities and govern his actions in accordance with the best interests of the whole. As it is now, the only people who obey the laws are those who cannot talk or buy their way out of trouble. For the Vietnamese this is a mark of class, and it is widely held that a man is a success in life when he no longer has to obey the laws.

Such attitudes are particularly characteristic of members of the elite, and as they fail to see their proper place in society, they also fail to understand why the war is being fought in the countryside. They sometimes oppose the war, as it interferes with business, and if they dislike the Viet Cong, it is for economic, not political reasons. They are interested in the peasant only as someone to harvest the rice, but they are not at all interested in doing anything to improve his life. Most feel that the peasant is a creature unworthy of their association or interest, and what few things they do for the peasant are done primarily to please the Americans. It is good business to keep the Americans happy.

There are, of course, some good officials and influential people who sincerely try to help the peasants—and their numbers are growing—but they are still too few to be of any great consequence, and their efforts are too often hampered by lack of support from higher levels. Many of these people with a sense of social responsibility are military men, and not true members of the moneyed and propertied elite. Many were born in the countryside and were able to rise in the military when other professions were not open to them. They have generally lived outside Saigon and they feel a close association with the people. In their military careers they have gained the education and political understanding necessary for them to be effective leaders, and if these people are given the guidance, support, and

**EQUIPMENT**   American M113 personnel carrier hit by a Viet Cong 50-caliber machine gun.

Vietnamese M113's bogged down where Viet Cong had cut the road **(above)**. M113's loaded with troops pull up to a village **(below)** and troops race into village **(right)**.

Two American A1E's loaded with bombs and napalm **(top)** fly over the South Vietnam countryside toward their target **(bottom).**

**SAIGON**

Crowd surges toward policeman at Buddhist self-immolation one week before the Diem coup in 1963 **(top)**. Grade school students **(bottom)** join the bloody student demonstrations that brought an end to the Khanh government in 1964.

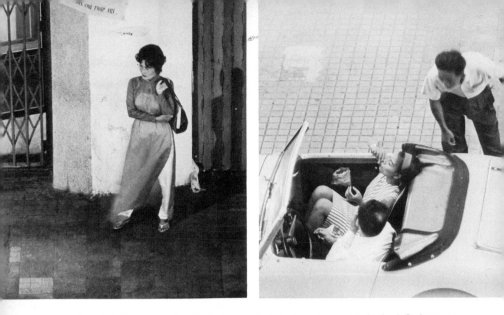

Prostitute waits for GI's **(top, left)**. Sports-car-minded Saigonese live completely apart from the war **(top, right)**. Black market display of some military equipment. Any item of U.S. military field gear can be bought on request **(bottom, left)**. Buddhist Boy Scouts and Vietnamese airmen move a statue of Buddha for a religious service **(bottom, right)**. Street demonstration in Saigon **(right)**.

**PEASANTS**

Peasants construct thatched roof on a typical peasant home **(left)**. Inside a peasant's home the pigs, an important means of livelihood, live with the family **(top)**. A Vietnamese soldier passes Buddhist monks in a village and an old woman prays before a typical family altar **(middle)**. An old woman carrying water passes American Marines resting on a trail **(bottom)**.

A Vietnamese mother cries as her home burns; a child looks longingly at the Vietnamese Marines' rice; and children mourn the death of their mother, who had not reached shelter when the attack on her village started.

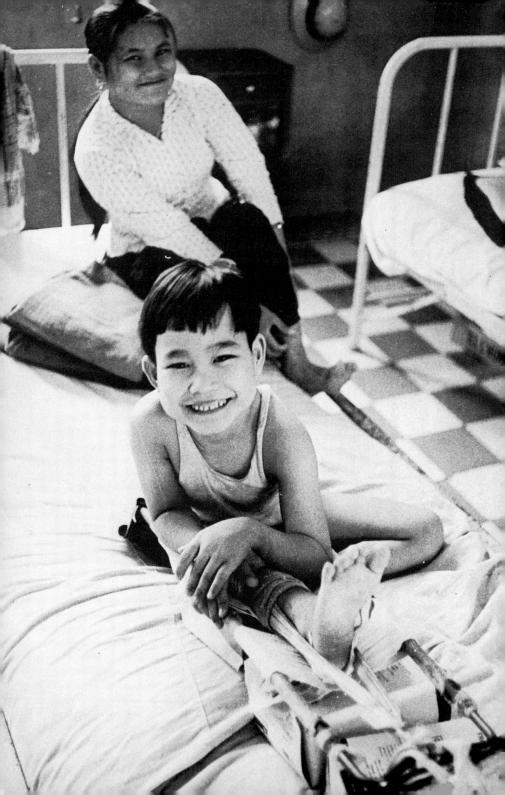

Young boy with a broken leg smiles in a USAID-supported hospital **(left)**. Health posters produced and distributed by USAID are plastered on the side of a country home **(right)**. Chieu Hoi's (Viet Cong returnees) are given a lecture by a USIS official in an effort to win their loyalty **(bottom, left)**. USAID field worker talks with an assistant outside USAID's Saigon headquarters **(bottom, right)**.

**AID**

Villagers receive pigs by helicopter as part of the program to increase pig production **(top, left).** Vietnamese-speaking USAID worker discusses with a Vietnamese farmer the value of spraying to control insects **(top, right).** Bridge built with USAID funds after the Viet Cong destroyed the former bridge **(bottom).**

**SUB-SECTOR ADVISOR**

Major Hai discusses Buddhism with Capt. Evans **(above).** Capt. Evans and soldiers in civilian clothes ride a civilian bus to avoid a Viet Cong ambush **(middle).** Capt. Evans points to the new school roof replaced with sub-sector funds after the Viet Cong destroyed the old one **(bottom).**

Capt. Robert D. Evans

Major Van Hai

SP4 Alvin L. Bacon

Sgt. George R. Parker

1/Lt. Fore, Capt. Evans' assistant, dunks the ball during a volleyball game with some of the villagers of Cai Lay. Volleyball is a favorite sport of the Vietnamese **(left).** Capt. Evans talks in pidgin Vietnamese to some of the children of Cai Lay **(bottom).**

# THE FRENCH WAY OF WAR

Even with our use of helicopters we are perhaps even more dependent on roads than the French were. Large convoys of troops and supplies are typical, and in a land cut by thousands of rivers it is all too easy for the Viet Cong to make a route impassable by dropping a span of bridge. Electrically detonated land mines are also used to slow a convoy for a short period. Small isolated outposts, many of them constructed by the French, are still manned even though they are almost totally ineffective as a defensive measure. There is wide spacing between homes in villages, making the total village perimeter so long that it becomes almost indefensible. Barbed wire fences around these villages are often poorly constructed and do not stop Viet Cong trying to enter the village.

time they need, they will someday turn South Vietnam into a nation ruled by the will of the majority. It is my opinion that in South Vietnam the traditional American fear of giving political jobs to military men may be unfounded.

Although there is corruption, thievery, naivete, and plain stupidity in Saigon, Americans have seen worse in other Asian countries. When we fought in the Philippines and in South Korea, corruption and thievery were much more prevalent than in Vietnam today, and while the Vietnamese are politically naive and have very little knowledge of the responsibilities of freedom, the fact that there is a growing number of dedicated officials, particularly among the military, is at least a step in the right direction.

# 9: COUNTRYSIDE AND THE MOTIVATIONS OF THE MASSES

"When the people are protected the regime will be secure."
Confucius
(seen on a village pagoda in the Mekong Delta)

Eighty percent of the population of South Vietnam consists of peasants or very small businessmen serving the peasants, and though the war is being fought to save these people from Communist exploitation, to most of them the future looks very bleak, no matter which side wins. The peasants only want peace and to be left alone. They are tired of living in constant fear that a military operation will be conducted near their villages and stray shots will kill their children. They are tired of having soldiers wander through their villages stealing chickens and rice. They are tired of having to pay taxes to both the government and the Viet Cong.

Life is hard for the Vietnamese peasants and they are overjoyed with little things like a good year in the fields, having enough clothes to wear, or a month without fighting in their village or without raiding parties coming to take their young men for military service. They would like better schooling for their children, health facilities, lower taxes, less work, and a chance for legal retribution if they have been cheated, but they have learned not to expect any of these things. Representatives from both the Viet Cong and the government promise all these and more, but very little ever comes from either side.

The peasant knows how to plant a successful crop. He can build a hut from bamboo and palm leaves and build simple machines and household gadgets with nothing but a knife and ingenuity. He can do things by hand that most Americans think are impossible without machines. He is a religious man in the sense that he believes in spirits and in the importance of paying proper homage to them. He respects and pays homage to his priests, be they Buddhist or Catholic, primarily because he feels they can intercede with the spirits in his behalf. He has a strong sense of family, but very little sense of community. If he lives along a canal he wants to have his property fronting on it; otherwise he feels he can't trust his neighbors to let him use the canal. He also likes to have as much space as is possible between his home and those of his neighbors, and he likes to have his fields near his home so he can keep an eye on them, and no one can take them away from him.

The land the peasant works is usually not his own and he must give a certain percentage of the harvest to his landlord. He also pays a heavy tax to the Viet Cong and a very small tax to the government. However, the Communists argue that the payment to the landlord is also a tax, and since it usually is the largest payment of all, and often set according to the landlord's whim, the peasant often feels it is less fair than the high Viet Cong tax.

Though there are laws to limit land rents and the size of holdings, landlords still charge pretty much what they think they can get, and at present there is no system of law enforcement that can stop them, especially in areas not securely held by the government. Most landlords with holdings in these areas live in the government-protected cities, and they go into the countryside to collect the rents whenever the area in which they have holdings is safe to visit. Usually, the opportunity comes when a government unit is operating in the area. For his protection, a landlord will often give a military commander a percentage of whatever he collects from his tenants, and a landlord will always try to get the most he can, as he never knows if he will ever get another chance to collect. Vietnamese military commanders sometimes feel justified in helping landlords collect the rents, as the peasants may not support the government, and therefore are thought to be as bad as the Viet Cong. To the peasant the rent is just another tax from which he gets no benefit, except perhaps to be left alone for another year. He has little concept of the principle that taxes should contribute to building the nation and to his own well-being. To them a tax is simply tribute paid to authority.

The amounts a peasant must pay to the landlords, the government, and the Viet Cong vary from time to time, but for as long as the peasant can remember, the end result has been the same. He is always on the border between bare subsistence and starvation, and after he has fed and adequately clothed his family he has nothing left. An endless cycle of poverty is his primary problem and he can't believe that any type of government is going to solve it for him.

The peasants generally live in groups of homes the Americans call hamlets. In a hamlet there are usually about a hundred families, with a population of five hundred to a thousand people, most of them being children. The typical hamlet is a single line of houses along the bank of a river or a canal, and nearly every home will front on the water, with a wide separation between the different houses. A hamlet may be only a hundred yards wide yet half a mile long. Other hamlets, built away from streams, may be circular in shape and contain a large number of rice paddies within the hamlet boundaries. The total perimeter around such a hamlet may be three to four thousand yards and if it is government controlled it will be fenced with a few interwoven strands of barbed wire. The fences are hardly a good deterrent to the Viet Cong, as any soldier could jump over or cut one of them in no time. There may be thirty or forty popular forces to defend a hamlet, but they are often away doing other jobs, and the Viet Cong have easy access to all but the most heavily fortified.

Hamlet boundaries, which were arbitrarily set a few years ago when the first strategic-hamlet program was started, may divide a line of houses along a canal into two or three hamlets, the one long line having been considered too difficult to administer as a single unit. Often, in areas where the government has no firm control, a peasant is not sure which hamlet he lives in.

If his hamlet is only a few miles from the town where the provincial market is held, a peasant may travel to it once or twice a month to buy clothes or some special food not sold in his hamlet. As most of his basic needs are provided for in his hamlet, he makes the trip infrequently to save the two or three cents he must spend for a round trip ride on a three-wheeled scooter. If a peasant's home is at a greater distance from the provincial capital, he may never go farther than his village headquarters.

Though hamlet government was introduced by the Americans, in the minds of the peasants the village is still the basic administrative structure in the country. Every peasant knows the name of his village, of which there are approximately twenty-six hundred, and each village has a headquarters, usually near a rice mill in which the crops of five or six hamlets are processed. In the headquarters there is a village chief who collects taxes, handles relations with other villages, and judges local disputes. The chief, who usually inherits his job, has the highest place of honor in the village. One mark of this importance is that the Viet Cong have systematically assassinated or kidnapped more than two thousand village chiefs in the past few years. Many village chiefs dare not stay in their headquarters at night, and move to the district or provincial capitals every evening. Those who do stay generally sleep in a different house each night.

The peasants have little knowledge of the world outside their villages, to the extent that many of them still think that Ngo Dinh Diem is president of Vietnam. One extreme example of the peasants' lack of awareness of anything outside their villages was observed about a year ago in a Mekong Delta province that borders on Cambodia. At that time Saigon was concerned about a series of border incidents that had occurred between South Vietnam and Cambodia, and the government prepared an elaborate four-color booklet outlining its case. Several thousand of these were dropped over Vietnamese villages near the border, and a few weeks later, an American advisor decided to make a survey of the effectiveness of the booklet. Before he gave up, he had questioned a hundred and twenty-three people, not one of whom knew there was a nation called Cambodia.

Today in South Vietnam, the peasants are faced with two alternatives: to support the Viet Cong or to support the American-backed South Vietnamese government. To a peasant the choice is extremely difficult. He knows the Americans bring aid, that they give him pigs, improved rice seed, and chemicals to kill the pests. Sometimes they dig wells, and build bridges and schools. On the other hand, the Americans have promised many things they have not delivered. It seems that for every one man who brings something, there are ten men who promise things that never come. Every month or so, Americans or Vietnamese government employees come into his hamlet and promise things like pigs and schools, but he is never sure they will arrive. Though the peasant recognizes that the Americans do many good things for him, there is always the question of when it will end. He is sure it will end if the Americans go away, and he is confused by the Americans' actions, as he does not understand why the Americans feel they should help him. Being gracious by nature, the peasant humbly accepts anything he is given but he always expects it to be the last. Some of the peasants hope the assistance will continue long enough for them to get on the road to an improved way of life, but only a few really expect it to last this long. A bridge or a school is very useful and makes life a little better, but it does not solve the basic problems of the peasants.

In their pacification and assistance projects, the American civic action teams move into the small peasant communities and try to tackle a succession of basic problems. First of all, after a community has been reclaimed from the Communist forces, the Americans and the government officials try to eradicate the remaining Viet Cong infrastructure, for if this isn't done, the community can never truly be pacified. As well, a system of fortifications must be laid out, and a local para-military force be recruited and trained to man it, or otherwise the VC can move right back in. Despite the busy activity that initiates the project, the peasants continue to have their doubts about its success, as they are aware that only some of the Communist sympathizers have been discovered and that the local force is too small and too weak to keep an effective watch over the defense perimeter. As to the fortifications themselves, as the peasants see that the obstacles and fences can't keep their children in, they have no reason to believe that the structures will keep the Viet Cong out, particularly as the Viet Cong regularly come at night to tear holes in the fences as a warning to those inside. And though the peasants have a radio to call for reinforcements in case of attack, they know that there is little chance that help will get to them before it is too late.

As the project gets underway, the Americans call for community elections. A big holiday is organized, and the peasants elect committees to deal with their problems, but though the committees meet and have discussions, the problems remain unsolved. Without the force of the government troops, rice cannot be moved to the mills or the markets, and the peasants themselves, no matter how they are organized, are unable to defy the Viet Cong who surround the community. The futility of the situation is not lost on the peasants.

This is not to say that the peasants welcome the arrival of Viet Cong in their communities, but it is true that the behavior of Viet Cong cadres is easier for them to understand than that of the Americans. In the first place, the Viet Cong arrive looking and acting like peasants, and though they tax the people heavily, they show that they understand the problems of peasant life. Unlike the government troops, they ask for what they want first, rather than stealing, and if they do not have money to pay for it, they at least sign a receipt. They have no ties with the hated cities, and they stay in or near the hamlets and help with the work in the fields. They even help with the household chores. If the government troops and their American advisors return, the Viet Cong leave, but they always return after the government troops depart and begin again to teach the people how to resist the government troops and how to avoid the damage of American bombs.

To the peasants, the Viet Cong make two kinds of promises. Some are small, like a promise to assist in the harvest or to help rebuild a home that has been hit by an American bomb. The peasants see that these promises are almost always kept, and in the evening, when the Viet Cong tell them stories of the beautiful life in the North, they cannot help but tend to believe the larger promises the Viet Cong make—those having to do with a Communist future.

Despite the concern the Viet Cong show for the everyday problems of the peasants, they are not soft hearted. As disciplinarians they are very harsh, and the people do not like discipline. Still, the Viet Cong are consistent and a peasant who has broken one of their laws knows why he is being punished. They may execute a peasant who has been caught giving information to government troops, but the peasant will have been told repeatedly that such behavior is punishable by death. The people do not like such harsh justice, but it makes more sense than when government troops come through the villages and torture and kill their friends for no apparent reasons.

As a unit of American troops approaches a village, the Viet Cong often provoke their fire by shooting a few rounds into their midst, and of course any casualties that result from the American fire are almost always innocent villagers. Although the villagers may be aware of the Viet Cong provocation, this does nothing to lessen their resentment of the Americans, particularly as they have been subjected to an endless lecture on American atrocities. Despite the rising number of Viet Cong who are killed by the increased American firepower, it must be remembered that more and more of the people are being killed as well. Such was also the case under the French, and as the attrition diminished when the French went away, a peasant can easily make the naive rationale that if the Americans were forced to leave Vietnam the people could begin to live in safety. After all, this is what the Viet Cong are forever saying. Then, too, the Viet Cong never stop saying that discipline and taxes are only temporary evils and once the National Liberation Front takes over these will be eliminated.

The villager does not think the Americans would have shot at him if the Viet Cong had not shot first, but then the VC tell him about American atrocities they have seen committed in other villages and the villager is not so sure about the American anymore. (The man who talks longest and last usually has the best chance of selling his propaganda. The Viet Cong always talk longest and last.)

The villager can see that despite all the American helicopters and bombers the Viet Cong have been getting stronger and stronger and their weaponry has been improving. They know that the Vietnamese government soldiers, if not getting weaker, are certainly not getting much stronger. They are well aware that all the added military firepower comes from the Americans, and will leave if the Americans ever leave. They also know that the Viet Minh beat the French (they have been told of the "heroic struggle" by the Viet Cong), and they believe that it is possible that the Americans could be defeated by the Viet Cong.

Many of the problems that arise in dealing with the peasants the Americans and the Vietnamese government have created themselves. They recognize the importance of providing security and control of population and commodities, but they are not willing to outline and enforce programs that will really do this because they are afraid the peasant will dislike them for being too strict. So they set up programs, but enforce them only to the extent that they don't irritate the peasant (or more accurately to the extent that they don't irritate the Viet Cong).

Part of the reason for this lack of enforcement is the small number and the poor training of the police and soldiers available to enforce these laws. But more important is the basic operating principle that nothing should be done to make the peasants angry. I witnessed a prime example of this type of thinking a year or so ago, and the basic reasoning has not changed since that time. In this particular case a group of Catholic villagers had been forced out of their homes by the Viet Cong and they decided to resettle near a wooded area a couple of miles from one of the government's regimental headquarters. One day they appeared with all their belongings and started building homes along the road. The military authorities watched while these people started building their homes with much space between each house and in one line over a half mile long. Most of these people were engaged in the profession of making charcoal and each man wanted to lay claim on a strip of timber behind his house which he could then use for making charcoal. A few weeks later the government came along and paid each family a resettlement allowance for moving out of Viet Cong territory and coming into that controlled by the government.

Nobody ever bothered to tell these people that they had constructed a hamlet that was probably more indefensible against the Viet Cong than the one they had left. Without having ever asked the peasants, the officials assumed that they would not want to build their homes close together, or in some configuration other than a straight line. They did not suggest that the only way these people could defend themselves against the Viet Cong, whom they obviously hated, would be to build their homes close together. They did not suggest that the government would only pay the resettlement allowance if the hamlet were built according to government standards. They did not offer to work out the problems of title to timber land by supplying each family with a deed to an equal share of timber property. They simply assumed that the peasants would dislike them if they suggested any changes. Also, they somehow thought that they had accomplished a very great thing because the peasants had left the VC and come over to the government side. This cannot be blamed on Vietnamese inefficiency because Americans were watching this project from the beginning.

On those few occasions when someone does decide that changes should be made, they generally issue an order that the peasants must obey rather than suggesting it in such a way that the peasant will decide that it is in his best interest to do exactly what the government wanted him to do in the first place. The peasant does not like the idea of government because it has never done anything for him, and a weak-willed, inefficient government is not going to change his attitude.

# 10: U. S. AID

The United States AID (USAID), a branch of the State Department's Agency for International Development, is the organization that provides funds and advice for all economic development in South Vietnam. This includes projects of immediate and short-term benefit, such as relief supplies, and long-range programs of "nation building," such as improvements in education and industry. All of the funds for such projects are funneled through the Vietnamese bureaucracy in an effort to train and give confidence to local officials.

On such programs USAID spent over three hundred million dollars in 1965 and will spend about five hundred and twelve million in 1966, but these figures are deceptive, as more than seventy percent of the funds—two hundred and twenty-five million in 1965—goes into a commercial import program designed to make available the commodities the country needs but cannot afford to buy for lack of international credits. Thus, the United States buys commodities such as fertilizer, pharmaceuticals, petroleum products, machinery and tools with dollars and ships them to Vietnam. When they arrive, Vietnamese importers pay their regular dollar value in piasters to the Vietnamese government, and in this way the importers get the products they need, and the Vietnamese government gets the money needed to run the country. However, as a Vietnamese importer has to pay for this product, he does not recognize that the United States government is doing him any favors. And as the Vietnamese government uses the money it gets to pay for the normal workings of the government—with the result that income taxes are extremely modest, ranging no higher than five percent—people do not realize that if it were not for this aid there would be no money to pay the salaries of the government employees and everyone would have to pay much higher taxes.

The economy of South Vietnam would immediately collapse if the Commercial Import Program were halted, but the real objectives of American aid activities must be more than those designed just to keep the basic economy going. The country, which is overwhelmingly agricultural, has to be given an increased industrial base if the people are to be able to produce and enjoy on any great scale the products of modern technology, and though they have very little to work with, USAID officials have so far accomplished quite a lot.

Local industries owing their development to American assistance now produce such diverse products as aluminum products, electric light bulbs, foodstuffs, paper, rubber tires and textiles. The local sugar-processing industry has been greatly expanded and material for fishnets is more readily available and the product more easily sold. In the five years ending in 1964, American-financed factories turned out products valued at one hundred and twenty-five million dollars, and in the same period some ninety thousand new jobs were created in the more than seven hundred factories that were built or expanded.

American aid to agriculture and fisheries has also shown results. Since 1955 there have been over three hundred trained agricultural extension workers put to work in the provinces and some five hundred Vietnamese have been sent abroad for advanced work in agricultural science. In addition to teaching the farmers better methods of crop management, officials distribute improved rice seed—eight hundred and thirty tons in 1964— and to date more than fifteen million piasters have been lent to farmers by the American-supported National Agricultural Credit Organization. Vietnamese farmers are using ten times the amount of fertilizer that they did a decade ago and their fields are yielding up to fifty-five percent more per hectare, and the nation's fishing fleet has added ten thousand motorized vessels to produce a far greater yield than before.

An ambitious American-backed public works program is building improved water and power systems in the communities. Rural electrification is progressing, as is the repair of roads and the enlargement of port facilities. To give stability to the cities, and to protect the movement of vital goods throughout the countryside, American funds help the government to recruit and train a national police force. In the 1965 budget, eight million dollars were given to this alone and the force now numbers some fifty thousand.

In education and health, American aid has led to significant advances. In 1955 there were three hundred thousand pupils in 1,189 elementary schools, and by the end of 1964 the numbers had risen to 1,215,000 pupils in 4,635 schools, and during the same period, the numbers of secondary schools and pupils quintupled. Three thousand regular teachers have been trained in the last ten years and over five thousand people undertook ninety days of training for which they received certification as hamlet school teachers. In the field of public health, more than seven thousand Vietnamese health workers are stationed in two hundred and twenty-five districts, and though they are often poorly equipped, there are now four thousand village and hamlet health stations.

These are only a sample of the projects the United States AID has been involved in, and though some of the accomplishments are impressive only because in some fields very little had ever been done before, the USAID officials have worked hard with considerable success despite what often seem to be insurmountable difficulties.

The difficulties USAID is having are not because people within the organization do not know what to do, but because the funds, the people, and the facilities have been too limited to allow them, at any one time, to devote a reasonable amount of effort to all the projects within their spheres of influence. They have had to set priorities giving emphasis to one thing now and something else later, and just as one project is going well, it is decided that attention must be given to something more demanding. According to some government sources, we are spending between twelve and twenty billion dollars in Vietnam this year and only eighty million of it is really going into something that could conceivably help the people. USAID people have done as much as possible with what they have been given, but they have only received a pittance of the amount needed. Despite the Honolulu Conference, a good hard look at the problems has not been taken. A little more has been added to the Commodity Import Program, but no more has been fed in to bolster the eighty million, a figure which should be closer to one or two billion.

In the closing months of 1965, the most common complaint of USAID men in Vietnam was that they had no supplies to work with. They had authorization to build schools, but no materials. In some provinces there were no relief goods available, and throughout the country stocks were low. USAID, which operates its own air transport force, was doing all it could to move supplies, but its air force was not large enough to do the job without assistance from military aircraft and military road convoys, and this was at a time when the military was having its own problems in moving supplies, and anything needed by USAID was at the bottom of the list of priorities. Of course, no one suggested that aid should be flown to the peasants before equipment was sent to the men in the field, but there is an overall question of how effective these military men can really be if there is not a steady flow of economic assistance to the people. However, in 1965 the strength of the United States military in Vietnam increased six fold to almost two hundred thousand, and it doubled again in 1966 to over four hundred thousand American troops. With this rapid increase it is unlikely that the supply problems will ever be completely solved and USAID will probably remain at the bottom of the list.

To help administer all its varied programs, USAID has approximately two hundred and fifty men living outside Saigon. Each province has a representative and most have an assistant. It is these men who must supervise all economic, social and political activities within the province, though many provinces also have a USAID doctor, or a specialist in agriculture, or public safety. Also, the USAID men in the field get assistance in the areas of information and propaganda from several hundred Vietnamese, advised by twenty-eight Americans who work for a branch of the United States Information

Service. All together, more than six hundred Vietnamese assist the USAID officials working outside the capital.

This might be considered an adequate number of administrators under normal conditions, particularly when the Vietnamese are meant to handle most of the administration themselves, but the time that must be devoted even to the smallest tasks, particularly at the provincial level, allows the average province representative to devote his attention only to a small percentage of the vast number of projects that are his responsibility.

For instance, not long ago a province representative stationed near the capital received a notice that some surplus furniture was available in Saigon and that any request for such furniture would be immediately approved, providing the requester could supply his own transportation for moving it. At that time, the province representative needed tables, chairs, and bookshelves for a district library he was trying to set up, so he immediately submitted a request in writing for some of the furniture. After waiting the usual number of weeks, and not having heard from Saigon, he decided to check up on his request. First he called Saigon, which is a time-consuming job in itself, as it is very easy for a man in the provinces to spend hours trying to get a single call through to the capital. When he finally got his call through, the people in the office had to spend quite a while looking for his request, but they did find it, and they assured him that everything was approved and he could send his people in to pick up the furniture any time.

This particular man had spent several months in Vietnam, and it all sounded a little too easy, so he decided to go to Saigon with the Vietnamese truck driver and his work crew. As it turned out, it was a wise decision. When he arrived in Saigon early one morning, it seemed that no one had ever heard of his request, but having learned to be aggressive, he dug around through the "in" baskets in the office until he found the request. As the request was still not signed by the proper officials, he decided to carry it by hand through all the necessary channels.

It was late afternoon before he was able to load the furniture, and it had taken him one entire day, not to mention the time involved in making phone calls and writing requests, to get a truck load of tables, chairs, and bookcases for one very small library, and this is by no means an unusual case. It is routine.

This particular province representative had a definite advantage in that he could drive to Saigon any time he wanted to, as there are only about six of the forty-three provinces from which a man can drive to Saigon with relatively little risk of ambush. In the other provinces, if the roads are open at all, a military convoy is needed for at least part of the trip; consequently, most province representatives and province chiefs are able to make very few trips to headquarters, and must rely on telephones, radios and the postal system as means of pushing their routine requests through the bureaucracy.

Getting furniture is only a routine supply matter when compared to the difficulties the province representatives encounter in trying to get supplies for the much-touted "self-help" projects, for it is on these projects that we depend most for winning the goodwill of the people. Under this program, the people of a hamlet can request materials for a bridge, a well, a school or almost anything else they think they need and can build themselves. Though they must complete one project before being allowed to submit a request for another, there is no limit to the number of projects they can undertake. For the Vietnamese administrator this type of project presents a difficult administrative problem, as very few general rules can be laid down on how much certain projects should cost, since each project is different in size and scope and the prices of materials and transportation vary in different areas. Each project has to be judged on its own individual merits.

Consequently, the people in the hamlets are told, "All you have to do is submit a request and you'll get your materials," but too often they submit their request and anxiously await arrival of the materials, while months pass and nothing comes. Then the people in the hamlet say, "the government is never going to do anything for us. It's like the VC say, the government is no good." Even after they get the materials they are still a little skeptical about whether the government will ever do anything else for them. As a result, these projects that are supposed to be building the people's confidence in their government often end up reinforcing the age-old belief that government can't be counted on.

Larger projects that require regular contracted labor are also running into difficulty because of excessive red tape and inflation. Bids must be taken for any such project and then, in nearly all cases, submitted to Saigon for approval. It is often difficult to get bidders in the first place as they would rather work on the bigger and better paying military projects, and once bidders are found and the bids submitted, it generally turns out that by the time the bids are approved in Saigon, prices for the materials have gone up so much that the contractor can no longer afford to work for the amount of original bid.

When anyone talks about bringing in more Americans to assist and advise the government and to help in administering USAID funds, there is always someone to cry, "We can't run their government for them. The Vietnamese have to learn how to do it themselves." (This used to be the argument for not bringing in U.S. combat troops, but that seems no longer to be a consideration.) It is not my opinion that we should do it for them, but I do think they need more advice and encouragement. After all, no one in the United States would take a man straight from college and make him vice-president of a company, yet, in effect, this is what we are doing in Vietnam, where everything is growing and changing rapidly, and the Vietnamese are being required to do things that are beyond their scope of training and experience.

The almost childish approach of many of the Vietnamese administrators has shown itself in the vital matter of distributing the funds for the "self-help" program. As late as October 1965 there were provinces that had not spent any of the Ministry of Rural Construction funds for self-help projects that had been handed over to the Vietnamese government by

USAID on January 1, 1965, and in nearly all provinces the spending of these funds was lagging far behind schedule.

In some cases, the funds had not yet been released by the ministry in Saigon. In others the funds had been released in Saigon, but the province chief thought he needed additional approval in order to use the funds on specific projects, and there was a breakdown in communications in trying to get this misunderstanding solved. Often the programs lacked flexibility, and the province chief was required to get additional approval in Saigon, which was always slow in coming. Also, many province chiefs found that once they had the proper approval, there were no materials available in the province with which to begin construction, and it was impossible to get these materials from Saigon.

Frequently, there was a Vietnamese somewhere in the chain-of-command who was simply afraid to spend the money he had been given. In his zeal to do an honest job, and to impress his superiors, he was trying to make sure that every project he spent money for was absolutely necessary and contracted at the absolute minimum that could possibly be paid. While he was not trying to abscond with the money himself, he usually had an excessive fear that the people below him were corrupt, and he would refuse to trust their decisions. Sometimes it seemed that he was happiest if, when his superior came to ask him what he had accomplished, he could reply, "Nothing, but here is all your money back, and I haven't wasted a cent."

For a long time Americans thought that the Vietnamese wanted complete control of their country and their bureaucracy, and so they made every effort to put everything in Vietnamese hands. Now, they have discovered that while the Vietnamese definitely want complete control, many of them do not want to accept the responsibilities that this control entails. They are much happier when an American has to co-sign an approval for something because if anyone ever questions the decision they can blame it on the American.

Two years ago there was almost no thought of putting large numbers of Vietnamese cadres into villages that had been cleared of Viet Cong and letting them advise the village leaders in methods of establishing an effective government. Now there is a project underway to put elite teams of sixty men—trained in politics, security, and economic development—into such villages and let them work to develop village government. Despite a crash training program, the people chosen for this job usually have little or no experience for the work, and are turned loose in a village with a minimum of American, or top-level Vietnamese, supervision. Yet it is sad but true that in this work, an amateur can do as much damage as the untrained American soldiers described in the first chapter, and it is only one example of jobs in which the Vietnamese will need constant supervision and advice while they are gaining experience. In ninety percent of the cases these people want and are glad to accept advice, if it is not given as an order.

Prior to sending combat troops to Vietnam in 1965, the military found that thirty thousand American advisors were needed to train and supervise the various military activities of the government forces. Someone must have decided that it is a much simpler task to advise civilians in charge of economic, political and social development, as there are less than a thousand civilian advisors for these aspects of the struggle now in Vietnam.

# 11: SUB-SECTOR ADVISOR

"I'm a soldier, but my job here has little to do with military operations. It is seventy-five percent political," Captain Robert D. Evans told me in November 1965. Captain Evans, as senior advisor in the provincial sub-sector of Cai Lay, commands one of the almost two hundred and fifty American advisory teams that since the summer of 1964 have operated in the county-like districts of South Vietnam's forty-three provinces. The previous November Evans and three other Americans—a lieutenant and two sergeants—arrived at Cai Lay, which is two hours southwest of Saigon by jeep, to begin their assignment as sub-sector (district) advisors. The map showed them that Cai Lay, which is in Dinh Tuong province, was in a key military position on Highway Four, the major supply route for the Mekong Delta, and halfway between two of the Delta's most important towns, My Tho and Vinh Long. The capital of Cai Lay district is a small town of twelve thousand people and it lies twelve miles north of the Mekong River and eight miles south of a Viet Cong safe area known as the Plain of Reeds. The district itself is used by the Viet Cong as a rest area and there are at least three VC battalions in the district at all times, and other Viet Cong units are always moving through the district on their way to combat areas.

"When we arrived there were very few SOP's (standard operating procedures) for the sub-sector advisor, and there still aren't many. In the early days no one was sure what could be done, but it was understood that the work would vary greatly depending on the conditions in a given district, and that advisors should be given a great deal of flexibility," Evans explained. As a beginning, Evans' team set up a small pre-fabricated house in the corner of a school yard and then started trying to get acquainted with the townspeople, but this proved more difficult than they had anticipated. Evans' team was the first group of Americans that had ever come to Cai Lay with the intention of staying, and they quickly discovered that the Viet Cong had done a very effective job of explaining the "evils of American imperialism." "If we went into a schoolroom wearing our uniforms, most of the students would get up and walk out. We discovered that if we wore civilian clothes they would at least stay long enough to listen to what we had to say," Evans said.

In those first days, the team members felt it necessary to carry weapons, but they still moved about the town, eating at the local shops, trying to learn the customs, and talking to anyone who would listen. Before long the aid projects got underway, English classes were started, and the people began to realize that Americans were not so bad as they had been told. Evans was also assisted by Major Van Hai, the present district chief, who soon arrived to take over control of the district from the former chief, and under his leadership the administration improved and the people began to have more confidence in the government. People from the countryside soon began to move into Cai Lay and the secured hamlets nearby until the number in the district supporting the government is now almost 33,000, or an increase of 10,000 since Evans arrived. An equal number continue to support the Viet Cong, and the rest of the 130,000 are "on the fence."

One thing that led to an increase in the number supporting the government was the re-capture in December 1964 of the town of Ba Dua which lies some seven miles south of Cai Lay and is the second largest town in the district. The operation against Ba Dua was first thought to be a routine mission to harass the Viet Cong, who controlled the town, and there was no plan to retake it. Nevertheless, after a fierce battle with the VC, the government forces found themselves in control of Ba Dua for the first time in several years, and it was decided to hold the town and turn it into a model hamlet.

The members of the sub-sector team remember the next month as a time when they got plenty of exercise. Almost every day dignitaries from the provincial capital, or from the different military headquarters in the Delta, or even from Saigon, would fly in for an inspection tour of Ba Dua. The sub-sector team and the district chief would get a radio message saying, "So-and-so is arriving at Ba Dua by helicopter in an hour. Meet him there." At that time the road between Cai Lay and Ba Dua went only about half the distance and they would have to walk the rest of the way. "They never offered to send *us* a helicopter," Captain Evans recalls. (The captain had to laugh when he read a recent newspaper article that criticized sub-sector advisors for spending all their time riding around in helicopters, and implied that these helicopters would be better used for military operations. Evans has been in a helicopter no more than five times during his entire year in Vietnam.) With the dignitaries came relief supplies for the population of Ba Dua and great promises of support for economic development. But as so often happens after dignitaries return to their headquarters, they either forgot about the promises or assumed that everything was automatically taken care of. It was the responsible people in the district who recognized that it would be impossible to develop Ba Dua if the road from Cai Lay were not opened and kept open, and it took several months to get the necessary equipment and a lot of hard work to rebuild the old French road, and it is still a daily problem to keep it open.

Recruiting troops to defend Ba Dua was also a problem. Normally, when a hamlet is set up, regular government troops are left in the area only long enough for men from the hamlet to be recruited and trained as a popular force. In Ba Dua there were no young men for this purpose, as the VC had already recruited them. Consequently, there has been a battalion of regular government soldiers stationed in the hamlet ever since December 1964, and there is little hope of being able to move these troops out for other operational duties and continue to hold the town. Still, the fact that the troops are there and that aid has been coming in—much slower than promised, but coming eventually—has led to an improved economic situation around Ba Dua and has encouraged many peasants whose farms are nearby to move into the hamlet.

With the exception of Ba Dua, the district chief has not made much of an effort to expand his area of control in the past year. Instead, he has tried to consolidate his holdings along two roads that cross in Cai Lay and split the district in quarters. In the areas he controls, he has given plots of land to refugees, built small roads in the hamlets, and started a few development projects to make life in the government-controlled areas more attractive. Major Hai has tried to convince the people that their futures are with the government, but he fully understands that this cannot be accomplished just by doing things for them. As Captain Evans says, "You don't necessarily gain anything by building schools. I know of schools built with U.S. aid that have Viet Cong teachers. Everything must be followed with proper publicity and propaganda."

One thing Major Hai puts great emphasis on is talk. He explains this aspect of his job in his broken but effective English, "Americans have much, but no talk. VC no have, but talk, talk, talk. We must talk." Much of Major Hai's day is spent going from hamlet to hamlet talking with hamlet officials, finding out what they need, explaining what he can do for them, and then seeing that these things get done. Major Hai is very effective with the people, and though, like most district chiefs, he is a Vietnamese Army officer, he has spent about six of his eighteen years of service working as a district chief in various parts of the Mekong Delta, and he is one of the most experienced in Vietnam. While he lays great emphasis on explaining to the people what their government can do for them, he has learned not to promise any more than he has to. As all people in his job quickly learn, many projects that he expects to be automatically approved get bogged down in paperwork and are held up for months, and often overly zealous and inexperienced district chiefs or sub-sector advisors end up doing more harm than good when they promise a hamlet chief to get him something in a week or a month, and find six months later that it still has not arrived.

Just getting to the people is a problem for Major Hai and Captain Evans. Most of the routes they must travel are more or less controlled by the Viet Cong and in order to stay alive they must always keep one jump ahead of them. "The VC don't want to hurt the population because they need their support. They are only interested in destroying us—the representatives of government authority," explains Captain Evans. For this reason, Major Hai and his advisors often travel in civilian vehicles, for by the time a Viet Cong sniper figures out who is in the vehicle it is too late to hit it. Naturally, a variety of vehicles must be used. While I was in Cai Lay, Major Hai decided to go to Ba Dua for "talk" and to allow SSgt. George R. Parker, the team's medical sergeant, to hold sick call. Before the trip, everyone was told to put on civilian clothes, and when the time came to leave, up rolled one of the local buses—a converted three-quarter-ton truck—that the Major had hired for the afternoon. Disguised by our civilian gear, Major Hai, Evans, Parker, a few popular forces bodyguards and I all piled into the bus and headed for Ba Dua. On other occasions Major Hai does use his personal car, a black Citroën, but this is a very common vehicle in Vietnam and the VC can't blow up every black Citroën that rolls down Highway Four. So by continuing never to let his movements fall into a pattern, and by making his decisions known only at the last possible moment, Major Hai will probably live to a ripe old age despite the fact that he is number one on the VC list for political assassination in Cai Lay district.

When Major Hai and Captain Evans are not traveling around the district they spend their time checking and re-checking on the requests for funds and materials they have sent to higher headquarters, and at this point teamwork between the district chief and the sub-sector advisor is invaluable. The Vietnamese and the Americans have identical and parallel chains of command, and if there is a tieup at some point in the Vietnamese command line, a message can be sent through the American chain to a high superior officer of the Vietnamese in question. In this way it is possible to reach such an officer without committing the gravest of military errors—"jumping" the chain of command. The idea, of course, is that everything be handled through the Vietnamese chain of command, but if this breaks down and the need within the district is critical, supplies or funds can sometimes be moved through the American chain of command to the sub-sector advisor.

A frequent emergency is that of homes and property being

destroyed by artillery or bombing. In normal channels, it can take years for the government to pay the claims arising from such damages, and of course during this entire time the property owner will go among his neighbors telling them how bad the government is. Captain Evans remembers one instance when the district chief received a rather large sum in payment for a house destroyed by bombing, and as it was suggested that a ceremony be arranged, all the people were brought together to witness the handing over of the money. At the ceremony, the recipient, a very old and poor farmer whose house had been destroyed about a year and a half earlier, looked at the money and said, "What is this for?" When he was told that it was for his house, he replied, "I don't need it now. I've already rebuilt my house. I needed it a year and a half ago when I had no money and somehow had to build a house." To help ease such sources of resentment, the sub-sector advisors in Dinh Tuong province were recently given a special 50,000-piaster fund for use in emergency situations, and Captain Evans can now pay such claims immediately.

The favored method of giving U.S. aid is the self-help project, as it leads the people to feel they have a stake in the project, and in getting them to work together, it develops some of the basic elements of democratic government. A problem can arise, though, when skilled labor is needed. Recently, Cai Lay had a school project that required the services of four masons and two carpenters for twenty days. Due to the shortage of skilled labor in the district, this requirement would mean that the local carpenters and masons would have to volunteer their services for the entire twenty days while regular day laborers would only be asked to take one or two days off from their normal jobs. The carpenters and masons simply could not afford to donate this much of their time. If they did their families would starve. Now, money from this special fund, which is called an "impress fund," can be used to pay for such special labor.

The district chief selects uses for the special funds and the sub-sector advisor controls the money, which he may use to pay for anything that is not normally given away through U.S. aid channels. There is no time limit on spending the money and a new 50,000-piaster fund will be provided as soon as vouchers are submitted to show how the original money was spent. At first, the U.S. aid officials were skeptical about letting so much money loose at such a low level and with so little control over its use, but now they seem to be impressed with the way the money has been spent. The success of the project may eventually lead to district chiefs having even more autonomy in deciding what programs should be carried out in their districts, and to a policy of stockpiling supplies in the districts. These are two changes that many sub-sector advisors feel are needed if the district chiefs are ever going to be able to develop a smooth-running self-help program.

Unlike many district chiefs, Major Hai feels that the political requirements of his job are at least as important as the military, and he spends more at "political action" than at "military action," and many of his military operations are actually conducted for political or propaganda purposes. He will send his troops to sweep through an area on the fringes of a government-controlled village while he and one of his lieutenants go to talk to the village chief and address the local population. On these trips he always stops at the local pagoda to pay his respects to the priests, for though Major Hai himself is Catholic, he has made a special point of learning about the Buddhist and Cao Dai religions and has gained the respect of many villagers for taking an interest in their particular customs and religions.

Captain Evans always accompanies Major Hai on these operations and carries a few thousand piasters from the "impress fund" with him. If they find people with legitimate gripes against the government, such as a rice paddy destroyed by armored personnel carriers or pagodas damaged by bombing, the claimants are paid on the spot. Because of the large number of Viet Cong in the province there is quite a bit of bombing, either in pre-strikes for troop operations or in free-strike zones. Major Hai says, "When there is bombing on operations, we should tell the people that bombs were dropped because VC shot. We no do. We no have enough men and material [for propaganda]."

Viet Cong taxes in the district run from ten to fifty times those of the government, and for this reason alone most people would prefer to support the government if they could only be assured of protection, but extending government protection to more people is difficult, as the Regional and Popular Forces in the district can do little more than secure the few areas they already hold. There are about a thousand Popular Forces in the district and two companies of regional forces with something less than three hundred men. There are twenty villages in the district and the government controls nine, in which most of the Popular Forces are based. The Regional Forces are stationed in Cai Lay as a mobile reaction force. In the whole district the VC have about an equal number of armed men.

The 7th Division, which has its headquarters in My Tho, the province capital, conducts many operations in Cai Lay district, but they are all search and clear operations. The troops move through an area for a day or two looking for Viet Cong and then move on to another area and for several months the peasants will see nothing more of government troops. The 7th Division does have one battalion of troops stationed at Ba Dua in an effort to hold the model hamlet, but for months they have been trying to figure out how to get the battalion back into regular operations without giving up the town.

The district's military operations are almost entirely of a defensive nature. The Popular Forces man fifteen outposts, mostly in defense of village headquarters, and nineteen watchtowers, most of which overlook bridges. While the Popular Forces do move out from these posts on patrol, the missions are purely defensive. Ba Dua and Cai Lay are the only two places in the district that the Viet Cong might have trouble in overrunning in a single night. There is no question in anyone's mind that the VC in the district have the capability to destroy any watchtower or outpost. It is believed that the only reason they don't overrun them is that they feel the objectives are not worth the price they would have to pay. In years past, when the VC needed weapons more than they needed men, they did overrun many small outposts throughout the country. Now, they seem to avoid such attacks unless they are sure of an easy victory. They have never been able to hold the outposts they overran, and previously just to get the weapons and ammunition in them was sufficient reason to justify the casualties they had to take. Thus, it appears that as long as Major Hai can keep his patrols mobile and his guards in the villages wide awake, he has a pretty good chance of keeping all his outposts and watchtowers, as the VC do not want to attack them any more unless victory seems assured. Captain Evans calls the Popular Forces the unsung heroes of the war. "They do more to win than anyone else, but they lack training and support. They are paid about ten dollars a month, which is barely enough to live on. They work day and night. They are poorly armed and poorly supplied. They are not even authorized to keep medical supplies in their outposts, but we try to see that they have a few bandages anyway. If they are attacked, they know there is very little chance of their getting reinforcements."

In a year's time the attitude toward the Americans in Cai Lay changed from hostility to friendship and support. Now there is a large attendance at the English classes conducted by the advisors every evening, and shop owners are friendly and stop the advisors on the street to converse with them in a mixture of Vietnamese and pidgin English about the weather and the latest town gossip. Today, Evans and his men average two or three dinner invitations a week from the town's leading citizens. In short, the people have learned from the presence of four Americans that we are in Vietnam to help the Vietnamese, and not, as the Viet Cong claim, to take over the country. They would never have learned this without the constant presence of the American advisors.

Captain Evans feels that his greatest setback came when he and his team were pulled out for three days. One week in the summer of 1965 they received what was believed to be reliable intelligence information that a Viet Cong regiment was massing to try to overrun Cai Lay. Higher officials decided that such an attack was likely and had a very good chance of being successful, at least initially. They also decided that the advisors should be pulled out for their own safety, and Evans was ordered to close the house and move his team to My Tho. "The townspeople watched as we closed the house and left with our belongings," Evans recalled recently. "They knew why we were leaving, and I knew they were thinking, 'Americans will help us as long as there is no danger, but when trouble comes they will let us take care of ourselves.' " Continuing, Evans said, "The attack didn't come off, and three days later we returned, but it was a long time before I could hold my head up when I walked through town. This really destroyed what we were trying to do here. I'm not brave, but I was sent here to do a job, and if they're not going to let me do it, then send me home to my wife and family."

Despite this setback, Evans' team was able to score a propaganda victory over the Viet Cong's claim that white Americans discriminate against all non-whites. The way this propaganda victory came about was unplanned, but there is no question that it has had its effect. The radio operator of the team is a young Negro, SP4 Alvin L. Bacon of Boston, Massachusetts. The medic, and the only other enlisted man on the team, is SSgt. George R. Parker of Daisy Versty, Mississippi. Parker, a tobacco-chewing country boy, claims he was a member of the Ku Klux Klan before entering the service fourteen years ago. "Until I came to Cai Lay, I'd never eaten at the same table with a Negro," Parker has said, but since he has been at Cai Lay, he and Bacon have become the best of friends, working together, going out to the local cafe for lunch or beers, or spending their evenings at the local theater. Their close association and true friendship has not been overlooked by the local population.

Captain Evans now feels that he gave very little advice during his year in Cai Lay. "Major Hai knows what is needed and how to requisition the things he wants. My job was mostly to ensure that he got what he asked for." In addition to trying to smooth out the bumps in the supply channel, Evans feels that a vital aspect of his job was to let the people of Cai Lay district know why we are in Vietnam. He is quick to point out, however, that other sub-sector advisors may be required to handle their jobs quite differently than he did because of different conditions within their districts. He also thinks the things he learned and reported to his superiors about the problems of running a district may help in developing programs that will be more effective in the future.

Situations like the one at Cai Lay prove that an American "shadow government" can be of value in helping their administrators manage a district more effectively. While serving as advisors they can see to it that the absolutely necessary functions of government are taken care of even if they have to do it all themselves. Though in most cases the Vietnamese people at the lowest levels are honest and sincere, they often just don't know how or where to begin, and if we had a hundred years or so, and no war, it would be nice to let them learn by their mistakes, but under the present conditions, neither we nor they can afford this luxury. Admittedly, it is difficult to develop a "shadow government" without stifling the will of the Vietnamese to continue to administer their country, but men like Bob Evans have proved it is possible and it may be the only road to success.

It is interesting to note that when American advisors were assigned no lower than the provincial, or sector, level it was said there were forty-three different wars in Vietnam. Now that we have district, or sub-sector, advisors it is said there are two hundred and fifty. If we ever put advisors in the villages there will be, by the same reasoning, 2,600 different wars in Vietnam. Maybe, if we get the struggle sub-divided into 2,600 wars and start looking at it from 2,600 different angles we will get something accomplished.

# 12: THE FRENCH WAY OF WAR

One of the clichés most often used by United States political and military planners in Vietnam is, "We won't make the same mistakes the French did." Unfortunately, this is not true, as any simple comparison of the American and French approaches to the war will show that most of the basic errors are being made again.

The French lost in 1954 basically because they fought a defensive war, trying to hold a system of bases and outposts and refusing to go into the jungles in small patrols and stay. They lost because they had poor intelligence, and because they placed undue reliance on air support. They consistently underestimated the enemy, and failed to do anything for the masses of peasants. And they always fought their battles where the Communists wanted them to fight.

The Americans are still fighting a defensive war. Their primary commitment is to defend their equipment and lines of supply, and the basic necessities—food, medicine and ammunition—are only a small percentage of the supplies. At any given time, at least one-third of our combat troops are tied up in the defense of bases and equipment, and those who do undertake operations in the field are far more dependent on their supply lines than are the Viet Cong. This is particularly true of air-mobile divisions, for despite their ability to move quickly, they require a hundred and fifty tons of supplies a day more than a regular division. The Viet Cong, who stick to the basics and train their men to get along without the extras, are able to supply their entire contingent of some two hundred thousand men with only twelve tons of supplies a day.

The Viet Cong have another advantage in that they maintain no bases that they are not prepared to give up. They may fight a bit harder to hold some than others, but there are none that they are not prepared to abandon if it is militarily expedient. Due to their general philosophy of war, they feel they can give up bases in this manner without a resultant political loss. As Mao Tse-tung has said, "Preserving oneself . . . is the basis of all military principles."

On our part, there are bases we feel that we cannot afford to lose, not so much because of their military value, but because of the political consequences of losing them. This position is exactly like that of the French in regard to Dien Bien Phu. There was no military reason why that position had to be held at all costs, and there was no military reason why the war could not continue if the position were lost. The mistake of the French military commanders was that they committed themselves to hold Dien Bien Phu at all costs and when they failed the people and the politicians at home lost confidence in them. Still, despite the French example, we have committed ourselves to hold certain base areas, principally those of Danang, Quang Ngai, Qui Nhon, Bien Hoa and Saigon. Though it is not likely that any of these places will fall, we are expending a staggering amount of manpower and matériel to see that they don't.

One position we have committed ourselves to hold is the An Khe valley, and in my opinion it might well become our Dien Bien Phu. Both areas are valley floors surrounded by heavily wooded hills through which the Communist troops can move undetected, and if North Vietnam were to decide today that An Khe was a worthy target, and that they were willing to commit to this target all the regular PAVN forces now in the central highlands of South Vietnam, and were also reconciled to suffering the casualties they took at Dien Bien Phu, they could conduct such a decisive a battle in An Khe within a year.

Our military men say, "they couldn't do it without artillery," but the Viet Minh moved artillery through the jungles to Dien Bien Phu and had three hundred pieces operating by the end of the battle, and claimed that they fired three hundred and fifty thousand artillery rounds during the fifty-four days the battle raged. It might take them a bit longer to move this number of pieces to An Khe, but it could be done. When they are told this, our military men say, "So maybe they could get artillery there, but we would knock them out with our air power," yet the French used air power—everything they had in Vietnam for fifty-four days—and it did not stop the Viet Minh artillery.

The fact that we have more advanced aircraft, and more of them, than the French had won't necessarily solve the problem either, as was shown at the battle of Plei Me, where American bombers pounded the hillsides for more than eight days and still received fifty-caliber machine-gun fire on every raid. There is no indication that the Viet Cong withdrew from Plei Me because their positions had been made untenable by air strikes, and no one should assume that a force as tenacious as the Viet Cong is ever going to be easily driven off by conventional bombing.

The military men also argue that An Khe could be reinforced easier than Dien Bien Phu as it is nearer to our other bases, and because we have more men available and better transport equipment, but if reinforcements are simply dropped into the An Khe valley they will have the same handicap that the French at Dien Bien Phu had in not being able to do anything of an offensive nature to counter the Viet Cong threat, and will simply have to sit in the defensive positions and try to slug it out successfully with the Viet Cong. (In this way, the French suffered 7,184 casualties.) Though Americans might try to send reinforcements over the mountains to hit the Viet Cong in the rear, as yet the American troops have not shown that they are very good at this sort of jungle operation and the seasoned Viet Cong jungle fighters could probably prevent their getting through.

In further considering a possible battle in the An Khe valley, one might ask, "Why couldn't a beleaguered American force simply be lifted out by air?" But then one must remember that only the men are air-mobile, and all the equipment and supplies, which were originally trucked in overland, would be almost impossible to lift out. In any case, American military commanders, just like the French before them, will almost never leave the field to the enemy. Even if thousands are lost and the battlefield is of little strategic importance in the first place, the Western commanders do not seem to be able to learn the value of strategic retreat. They are determined to hold their positions, and even if the Americans, in a major battle at An

Khe, could inflict several times the number of casualties on the Viet Cong as they might take themselves, a loss like that the French suffered at Dien Bien Phu would surely be counted a victory for the other side.

In other aspects of the war, the Americans seem to be repeating the mistakes of the French. Though the Viet Cong are as much at home in the jungle areas of central Vietnam as fish in water, neither the French nor the Americans seem anxious to learn the requirements of successful jungle warfare. As one can read in the newspapers, American units are operating every day in the jungle, particularly in War Zone D and the Central Highlands, but the problem with these actions is that the troops go into the jungle in units that are too large and they don't stay long enough to accomplish anything. About the only contacts with the enemy that the Americans make when they move through the jungle are when they walk into ambushes or those rare occasions when they catch the Viet Cong napping, and though the Americans often make a good showing in these ambushes and kill a lot of Viet Cong, it should be remembered that the battles are being fought on terms set by our enemy, and until this can be corrected, the Americans will continue to fight a defensive war.

One way to change this would be to improve our intelligence-gathering facilities—a fact the military commanders fully recognize—but this is much easier said than done. We are not going to get much cooperation from the civilian population until we can offer them some measure of protection and security, but if we can offer them protection and security, they will no longer have much contact with the Viet Cong. If we could infiltrate the Viet Cong units with Vietnamese from our side it would probably improve our intelligence gathering, but as these people would have tremendous difficulties in passing information back to us, such a project on any major scale would be impractical. Though the only real alternative seems to be a large number of small reconnaissance patrols, this idea has never gained much favor in Vietnam, either in the French time or now. Most military planners think it is too dangerous to send men out in such small and vulnerable units; however, it is my opinion that if they were to question members of Special Forces "D" teams or Reconnaissance companies as to their preference for small or large patrols, they might get some surprising answers, particularly if the men have ever been on a company or battalion-size combat operation in jungle terrain. After all, it is very demoralizing never to see the enemy until he is shooting at you, and large units never do.

The Special Forces "D" Teams and the Reconnaissance companies of some of the major units are the only American elements that have a reasonable chance of surprising the Viet Cong, yet they are a pitifully small percentage of the total force in Vietnam. (The French also had a few specialized units that undertook this type of patrol, but they were never given much consideration, and as a result accomplished little.) To be effective, these units would have to number in the thousands, each spending a week or two at a time in the jungle and operating in an area small enough to get to know well. Most of these patrols would not produce any intelligence of great value, particularly in the early days of the program, and many men would be killed. The statistics released by the Pentagon would not look so good, as there would not be many major battles in proportion to the actual number of troops in the field. To set up such a program would be tantamount to saying, "We are fighting for a foothold in a very difficult war in which we will be losing a lot of men for many years. Although we are setting up programs that may seem unproductive at first, they will pay off in the long run—the very long run." Our government and our military are not ready to say such things. The French never were either.

Depending only on large operations, it was the French who were first caught in the trap of not wanting to grant the enemy any free zones of operation. Thus, whenever the Viet Minh began to mass in a particular area, the French would attempt to move a large force into the area to disperse it. They would do this without considering the difficulties of fighting in the area or its strategic value. As a result, they usually walked into a Viet Minh trap or, at the very least, were forced to fight on the enemy's terms, and the American forces in Vietnam are now doing exactly the same thing. During 1965, most of the operations in War Zone D and the jungles of the Central Highlands have been of this nature.

Unfortunately, these operations are like sweeping water with a broom. The water moves out of the way while the broom is there, but it comes rushing right back as soon as the broom is removed. Into the jungle areas, we have taken large units many times, and on a few occasions we have killed a large number of Viet Cong. But in looking back over the year, one can see that the Viet Cong still have free access to all the territory they ever had. We have not reduced their total numbers at all, and, in fact, they have constantly been on the increase throughout the two years I have spent covering the war. (Military sources estimated that there were over 200,000 VC in South Vietnam at the end of 1965 though these same sources had estimated the VC strength at less than 30,000 after the Diem coup in late 1963.) In our operations we have used a lot of supplies, lost a lot of men, and kept a lot of others occupied who might have been able to make better use of their time. Like the French before them, Americans have not learned that these one-shot operations into enemy-held territory—spending a few days and then not returning again for six months—do not accomplish a thing.

Such tactics seem especially useless when we consider that we are using so much of our energy to hit the enemy in areas where he can accomplish very little even if he is left alone. Few people live in the jungles, and the first and most important need of a guerrilla is people. Therefore, if the Viet Cong can be kept in the jungles and away from the people their effectiveness is severely curtailed. If the energies we waste in this manner were used to provide some added security in the populous areas we might accomplish something, but by allowing the Viet Cong to induce us to fight in the jungles we keep our forces away from the people and give the Viet Cong political cadres a chance to work undeterred.

Though we have probably done more to help the people of Vietnam than the French ever did, what has been done is so far below the amount needed to show any tangible results that for all practical purposes it is insignificant. The basic knowledge of what needs to be done is there, but this, like long-range patrolling, fails to get the support necessary to set up an effective program. As has been shown, much of the aid now given is of a relief, or one-shot, nature that does nothing to help the population build a workable economic and political system.

The prevailing attitude is that these things will come after the military situation is stabilized, but it is precisely for this reason that the military situation will not stabilize. The military commanders strongly resist getting the average GI involved in this type of program, or even training him to understand it, and yet the only men available for the work, and the only men who could work in most of the areas where assistance is needed, are military men.

The French, too, tried to keep their units separate from any political action. The Viet Cong, on the other hand, have as many as forty thousand political officers, with the power to veto any military order, who serve in every unit of their forces down to the platoon level. These men also have the responsibility for selling the Communist propaganda line to the peasants, and our efforts to counter this propaganda are negligible by comparison. They sell their line in personal contacts, while we try to counter it by dropping leaflets from airplanes.

Many military strategists were encouraged in 1965 when the Viet Cong began to mass and fight in big units, and these strategists are convinced we can beat the Viet Cong if they will only continue to stand and fight. However, in their enthusiasm over recent victories the strategists overlook history —specifically, the events of 1951 in North Vietnam. In that year General Giap's forces were severely beaten in at least three major battles, all larger than any battles we have had in South Vietnam to date. At that time, the Communists believed they could take on the French and win, but when they suffered major defeats, they pulled back, built up their forces, and allowed the French to wear themselves out. It seems to me that exactly the same thing is happening in South Vietnam, and I think the Viet Cong can be expected to pick their battles more carefully in the future.

The argument that the French were a colonial power and that America is not means very little to the peasants, as the results for them of French colonialism and the American presence in Vietnam have been just about the same. The one thing the U.S. does not seem to offer, any more than the French did, is relief from exploitation, and to peasants it makes very little difference whether they are being exploited by Frenchmen or rich Vietnamese. Too often, in the peasants' eyes, the Americans only seem to bolster a new class of exploiters, and though they do not understand that the Viet Cong, if they come to power, will probably exploit them too, they can only judge the people in power at the moment.

It seems then that we are using exactly the same tactics that the French used more than ten years ago. We may be going at it in a bigger way, but if it was the tactics themselves that brought about the French defeat then all our greater force will only prolong the inevitable and lead us to a bigger fall.

# 13: WHERE DO WE GO FROM HERE?

The discouraging part about writing this book is that it all has been said before, and yet no one seems to be listening and it is a foregone conclusion that no one will be listening now. Almost every newspaper and magazine writer in Vietnam has at one time or another made mention of these glaring faults. They have pointed out that the military "book" is not working, but there is every indication that the military men intend to stick to the "book," and claim to their last dying breath that it is right. We have come to a point in warfare and social development where great and controversial innovations are needed, but all our leaders seem to be doing is looking for consensus. It is almost comical, if it were not so tragic, to watch American commanders use and praise exactly the same tactics that a year ago American advisors criticized the Vietnamese for using. When the only Americans in Vietnam were advisors, a few innovations on standard "book" tactics were tried, but when the American commanders and American combat units arrived everyone quickly reverted to the old-line tactics that had worked in World War II and Korea.

These World War II tactics can only lead us to one place —China. The theory seems to be that if we cannot fight the war as it is, we must change it into the type of war we can. China does not want to fight, and will do everything she can to avoid it, as she has enough other problems at the moment, but we are going to end up forcing her to put her divisions into action against us because this is the only way our military men know how to fight a war. In spite of all the talk about not wanting to take on China, that is exactly where our military is headed. There is every reason to believe that before this book is published we will be in an air war—jets fighting jets—with the Chinese over North Vietnam. The Chinese simply cannot stand by and watch us pound North Vietnam to a pulp without eventually reacting. After we have suffered through the air war and decimated North Vietnam, none of which will do the least bit to stop the war, someone will decide that we must attack Chinese industry.

Of course, even if we eventually manage to win such a war

with China we still will not have solved any of the major problems of the Vietnamese, any more than we solved the problems of the Chinese with our victory in 1945. Americans prefer to spend their time arguing that Asians have to learn to govern their countries themselves and that we cannot do much for them, rather than really exploring the possibilities of what we can do to help them learn how to govern themselves. In the end, we waste a lot of manpower and money without ever getting to the crux of the problem.

It might be useful to estimate the extent of waste that we are likely to see in the next few years, and I would like to take election day, 1968, as a target for my predictions. We will surely be fighting in Vietnam on that day, and we will have increased the present 200,000 American troop commitment to over 500,000. At some point between now and then the total number of Americans will have gone well above this half million figure, and if the number is decreasing at that time, it will be because we are preparing to negotiate a defeat for ourselves. Over 15,000 Americans will have been killed (1,300 now) and 60,000 wounded (8,500 now). Billions of dollars will have been spent. This is our absolute minimum military commitment, and the road beyond 1968 is a long and difficult one. But unless we have changed our tactics by that time we will be no closer to victory than we are now.

Peace before November 1968 is impossible. The Communists are still convinced they can win in Vietnam, and it will take us at least three years to get programs going that might convince them otherwise. No amount of brute military force, except possibly the atomic bomb, which I do not advocate using, will convince them. Only effective political and social development in the countryside might change their minds, and getting such programs going is a slow process at best. Any truce or negotiated settlement before 1968 would be another Munich, and as Churchill said after Munich, "The belief that security can be obtained by throwing a small state to the wolves is a fatal delusion." If and when we ever get to a conference table on terms that might be at all favorable to us, the negotiations themselves will certainly take years.

While I think it is still possible to win in South Vietnam, realistically, I must say that it is not likely. If we were to concentrate the activities of our forces on protecting and gaining the respect of a certain small percentage of the people for whom we can provide a relative degree of security, and use guerrilla operations to harass the VC in the rest of the country, we might, over the long haul, be able to win. The war needs to be escalated, but in South Vietnam, not outside, and in the direction of economic improvement within the country. There is every indication that we intend to escalate in the opposite direction.

In this day and age of mechanization and automation we have finally found one place where only men can function well. This war requires highly trained and skilled individuals, using their brains more than their brawn, and operating as individuals or in very small groups. It requires that their work be not only in the military field, but in the political and social fields as well. Yet this is not the direction in which we are headed.

We will lose in Vietnam, not because it was inevitable from the start, but because we failed to think and change with the times. We will never develop our own effective American guerrillas. We will not train the average soldier well enough or keep experienced men in the theater long enough. We will continue to try to do the job with money and machines instead of men. We will always place military action above economic and political development. It is for these reasons that we will lose.

Also, the fact that we keep saying we are winning will eventually begin to defeat us by destroying public confidence in the government and the military. The years will go by and the public will begin to wonder why, if we are always winning, the situation never seems to improve. This more than anything else defeated the French, and it will probably defeat us. One can always find progress and it is certainly true that we have made some progress in Vietnam. In fact, if we take January 1965 as a base we could probably say that there had been 100 percent improvement by December 1965. Not bad for one year, but on a mathematical scale this is like saying that we have gone from 1 to 2, and we still must reach 100 or possibly 1,000 before we achieve what we are looking for.

If we are lucky, after we lose in Vietnam we will learn from our mistakes, and not make the same mistakes in the next country we go to, but there would certainly be more ground for optimism if we corrected a few of these mistakes before Vietnam is lost.

The Chinese philosopher Sun Tze once said, "Know your enemy and know yourself and you can fight a hundred battles without disaster." Not understanding the enemy is bad enough, but our greatest fault is not understanding ourselves. We Americans are not willing to admit and to correct our weaknesses in fighting guerrillas.

We may be the strongest nation in the world, but as yet we have not developed the ability to cope with guerrilla war. At one time Goliath was the strongest man in the world, but little David knew how to cope with him. David defeated Goliath because the big man was not smart enough to realize he could be defeated.

# INDEX

Quang, Dang Van, 25-6
Quang Ngai, 112
Qui Nhon, 112

Rangers, Vietnamese, 18, 24

Saigon, xvii, 7, 13, 25, 33, 58,
    59, 71-7, 82, 92, 93, 94,
    96, 99, 100, 112
7th Division, 106
Special Forces, 37-43, 67; "A"
    teams, 39-42; "D" teams,
    115; Reconnaissance
    companies, 115
Strategic Air Command
    (SAC), 66-7, 68-9
Sun Tze, 124

Tan Hiep, 17
Tan Uyen, 7
tanks, 57, 58-9, 60
troops, U.S., 1-9, 25-6, 59, 61

troops, Vietnamese, 23-7

UH-1B (Huey), 52
USIS, 92-3
USO, 17

Viet Cong, xii, xiii, xiv, 1, 2,
    3-4, 5, 7-8, 11-20, 24,
    25, 26, 37, 38, 39, 40,
    41, 45, 46, 47, 48, 49,
    50, 51, 52, 53-4, 58, 59,
    62, 63, 64, 65, 66, 71,
    76, 79, 80-81, 82, 83,
    84, 85, 86, 87, 95-6, 97,
    99, 100, 101, 102, 103,
    105, 106, 107, 108, 111,
    113, 114, 115, 116, 117,
    118, 123
Viet Minh, 19, 86, 112, 115-16

War Zone D, 7-8, 18, 114, 116
Westmoreland, 33
World War II, 9, 62, 63, 121